About This Book

Why is this topic important?

Despite the myriad benefits that e-learning can provide, high development and implementation costs leave many organizations out in the cold. Employees are denied opportunities for growth and pulled away from work to attend live training that could be more effectively provided by other means, while organizations continue to expend time and energy on instructor time, classroom space, and travel expenses. This is the first book devoted exclusively to helping organizations identify low-cost ways of delivering e-learning solutions.

What can you achieve with this book?

You will feel both encouraged and empowered that quality e-learning solutions are within the grasp of even the smallest organizations with the most limited resources. Take-aways include solid ideas for building solutions at minimal cost, strategies for negotiating reasonable expenses for "store-bought" e-learning products, and ideas for assembling tools, techniques, and strategies into workplace solutions. You will learn:

- How to confidently make the buy-or-build (or both) decision
- How to take inventory of existing resources (you'll probably be surprised—you likely have more than you think)
- How to use inexpensive e-learning solutions to fill in gaps between formal training events: bring about learning *in* work, not just learning *at* work
- How to find free, or almost free, design enhancers and interactivity tools
- How to recycle, reuse, and repurpose resources
- How to create engaging online training at a minimal cost
- How to build collaboration through creative use of free or low-cost technologies and techniques
- How to negotiate with vendors of off-the-shelf and custom content
- How to maximize your investment in a learning management system—if it's an investment you really need to make
- How to assemble tools and strategies into complete online programs

How is this book organized?

The book consists of three parts: creating e-learning in-house, which covers such topics as building and enhancing basic programs and creating low-cost collaboration; buying e-learning courses and custom content, which covers such topics as considering all the costs involved, knowing your criteria, and working with vendors; and putting solutions together to create robust e-learning programs.

"*e-Learning Solutions on a Shoestring* should be required reading for any organization considering an e-learning program. Jane Bozarth has done much of the groundwork for us by reviewing and prioritizing resources and filling her book full of ways to save money—a tremendously practical and useful guide."

—Colleen O'Connor Grochowski, assistant dean for curriculum development, Duke University School of Medicine

"Jane Bozarth's straight-shooting, can-do style gives hope and encouragement to those left out in the cold by high development costs. Proving that quality e-learning solutions are within reach, *e-Learning on a Shoestring* is the real deal for organizations trying to work with few or no resources."

—Nancy Gustafson, manager, organization effectiveness, First Citizens Bank, Raleigh, North Carolina

"If you are starting to develop a plan for the e-learning future, I can't think of a better place to begin than with this book. It provides the nuts-and-bolts tools that could change any training organization dramatically, and for the better."

—Kyle Hoffman, senior project manager, Institute for Human Services

About Pfeiffer

Pfeiffer serves the professional development and hands-on resource needs of training and human resource practitioners and gives them products to do their jobs better. We deliver proven ideas and solutions from experts in HR development and HR management, and we offer effective and customizable tools to improve workplace performance. From novice to seasoned professional, Pfeiffer is the source you can trust to make yourself and your organization more successful.

Essential Knowledge Pfeiffer produces insightful, practical, and comprehensive materials on topics that matter the most to training and HR professionals. Our Essential Knowledge resources translate the expertise of seasoned professionals into practical, how-to guidance on critical workplace issues and problems. These resources are supported by case studies, worksheets, and job aids and are frequently supplemented with CD-ROMs, websites, and other means of making the content easier to read, understand, and use.

Essential Tools Pfeiffer's Essential Tools resources save time and expense by offering proven, ready-to-use materials—including exercises, activities, games, instruments, and assessments—for use during a training or team-learning event. These resources are frequently offered in looseleaf or CD-ROM format to facilitate copying and customization of the material.

Pfeiffer also recognizes the remarkable power of new technologies in expanding the reach and effectiveness of training. While e-hype has often created whizbang solutions in search of a problem, we are dedicated to bringing convenience and enhancements to proven training solutions. All our e-tools comply with rigorous functionality standards. The most appropriate technology wrapped around essential content yields the perfect solution for today's on-the-go trainers and human resource professionals.

www.pfeiffer.com

Essential resources for training and HR professionals

E-LEARNING SOLUTIONS ON A SHOESTRING

E-LEARNING SOLUTIONS ON A SHOESTRING

Help for the Chronically Underfunded Trainer

Jane Bozarth

Pfeiffer

A Wiley Imprint

www.pfeiffer.com

Copyright © 2005 by John Wiley & Sons, Inc.

Published by Pfeiffer
An Imprint of Wiley
989 Market Street, San Francisco, CA 94103-1741
www.pfeiffer.com

For additional copies/bulk purchases of this book in the U.S. please contact 800-274-4434.

Pfeiffer books and products are available through most bookstores. To contact Pfeiffer directly call our Customer Care Department within the U.S. at 800-274-4434, outside the U.S. at 317-572-3985, fax 317-572-4002, or visit www.pfeiffer.com.

Pfeiffer also publishes its books in a variety of electronic formats. Some content that appears in print may not be available in electronic books.

Library of Congress Cataloging-in-Publication Data

Bozarth, Jane
   E-learning solutions on a shoestring: help for the chronically underfunded trainer / Jane Bozarth.
      p. cm.
   Includes bibliographical references and index.
   ISBN-13 978-0-7879-7712-2 (alk. paper)
   ISBN-10 0-7879-7712-8 (alk. paper)
  1. Employees—Training of—Computer-assisted instruction.
  2. Employees—Training of—Data processing. 3. Internet in education.
  I. Title: E-learning solutions on a shoestring. II. Title.
   HF5549.5.T7B62   2005
   658.3'12404'0285—dc22

                                 2005016227

Acquiring Editor: Lisa Shannon

Director of Development: Kathleen Dolan Davies

Developmental Editor: Susan Rachmeler

Production Editor: Nina Kreiden

Editor: Bev Miller

Manufacturing Supervisor: Becky Carreño

Printed in the United States of America

Printing 10 9 8 7 6 5 4 3 2 1

To my husband and love of my life, KENT UNDERWOOD: Thanks for always keeping up.

Contents

List of Tables and Figures xvii

Acknowledgments xxi

Introduction: Getting the Most from This Resource 1

Chapter 1 e-Learning: Some Basics 9

What Is e-Learning? 9

Why Use e-Learning? 10

Moving from Classroom to Online 11

Some New Ways of Thinking 12

Avoiding Costly Mistakes 14

Using e-Learning: Buy Off-the-Shelf or Build It Yourself? 16

Summary 18

PART ONE: DOING IT YOURSELF

Chapter 2   Getting Started with Doing It Yourself 21

Take Inventory: You Probably Have More Than You Think 21

What Else Should You Have? 23

User Considerations 24

Want versus Need: What Will Meet Your Objectives? 27

Summary 30

Chapter 3   Building Simple Pages and Programs 31

Using What You Already Have: MS Office Products and MS Paint 32

Time to Move Up? More Advanced Design Tools 49

Summary 54

Chapter 4   Enhancing Basic Programs 55

Free Clip Art and Other Media 55

Free Design Templates 56

Free Interactivity Tools 58

Free Microsoft Downloads 59

Macromedia Coursebuilder 63

Design Tips and Tricks 65

Summary 68

Chapter 5   Creating Inexpensive Quizzes, Games, Searches, Puzzles, and Simulations 71

Quizzes 71

Games 80

Searches: Treasure Hunts and Web Quests 89

Puzzles 94

Simulations 96

Summary 97

Chapter 6   Creating Low-Cost Collaboration 99

Synchronous or Asynchronous Collaboration? 99

Synchronous Tools 101

Asynchronous Tools 103

Creating Collaborative Activities 105

Summary 114

Chapter 7   Creating Performance Support Tools on a Shoestring 115

When to Use Performance Support Tools 118

Which Tool to Use 120

Performance Support Tools: Some Examples 120

Summary 124

Chapter 8   Leveraging Resources 125

Sharing 125

Networking 128

Bartering 129

Inexpensive—and Possibly Free—Help 129

Repurposing and Reusing 130

Summary 133

PART TWO: BUYING YOUR SOLUTIONS

Chapter 9   Paying Someone Else to Build for You 137

What Are You Buying? 138

How Much Does It Cost? 138

What Affects Costs? 139

How to Save on Costs 141

Beware of Hidden Costs 142

Doing Business: The Bid and Request for Proposal Process 143

Choosing a Vendor for Developing Custom Content 145

Summary 147

Chapter 10 Buying Off-the-Shelf Courses 149

Déjà Vu: Buy or Build? 150

Know Your Criteria 150

Customizing OTS Products by Adding On, Not Renovating 151

Tips for Working with Vendors of OTS Products 153

The Portal Alternative 156

Summary 158

PART THREE: PUTTING IT ALL TOGETHER

Chapter 11 Hosting Your Programs and Tracking Learner Data 163

Hosting 163

Tracking Learner Data 164

Moving Up: Do You Need a Learning Management System? 169

Tracking: A Recap 174

Summary 175

Chapter 12 Application 177

Mixing It Up: Matching Approaches to Learners and Learning Styles 177

Cases: The Buy-or-Build Decision 179

Cases: Assembling Tools and Approaches to Create
e-Learning Programs 182

Summary 186

References and Other Sources 189

Additional Resources 193

Index 199

About the Author 207

List of Tables and Figures

Tables

1.1 e-Learning or Classroom Decision Criteria 11

2.1 Inventory Checklist 22

2.2 Technology Assessment 24

5.1 Advantages and Disadvantages of e-Mail Games 81

6.1 Comparison of Asynchronous and Synchronous Approaches to Collaboration 100

7.1 Situations Appropriate for Use of a Performance Support Tool 118

7.2 Guidelines for Choosing a Job Aid 120

9.1 Outsourcing Development: Choosing a Vendor 145

11.1 Comparison of Must-Have Benefits versus Nice-to-Have LMS Features 171

11.2 Finding Solutions to Problems 175

Figures

1.1   Buy-versus-Build Flowchart 17

2.1   Sophisticated Multimedia Heart Sounds Tutorial 28

2.2   Clickable Heart Sounds 29

2.3   Illustrated Clickable Heart Sounds 29

3.1   Components of a Typical Course Created in PowerPoint 33

3.2   PowerPoint Action Buttons 34

3.3   Text Box Programmed to Hyperlink to Another Slide 35

3.4   Programming an Animation 36

3.5   Selecting an Animation from the Drop-Down Menu 37

3.6   Recording Narration by Clicking "Slide Show—
      Record Narration" 38

3.7   Selecting Quality of Recording 38

3.8   PowerPoint Show Saved as a Web Page 41

3.9   Example of a Word Web Page Wizard Layout Template 42

3.10 Course Main Page Created with Word Web Page
      Wizard Template 43

3.11 Sample Page of Course Created with Word Web Page Wizard 43

3.12 Examples of Form Tools Inserted in a Word Web Page 45

3.13 Saving a Word Document as a Web Page 45

3.14 Original Clip Art Image 47

3.15 Image After Editing with MS Paint 47

3.16 Screen Shot Created with MS Paint 48

3.17 Sample Home Page from Free Virtual Community Site 53

4.1   Some Free Web Page Templates Available from Elated.com 57

4.2   Online Agent Incorporated into Tutorial on
      Employee Timekeeping 60

4.3   Using MovieMaker to Break Video into Clips 61

4.4   MovieMaker Storyboard Showing Rearranged Clips and
      Added Titles 62

4.5   Example of a Coursebuilder Slider 64

4.6   Slider Interaction 64

4.7 Use of Metaphor in an Online Training Program 66

4.8 Example of a Site Sampler 67

4.9 Text Is Revealed as Mouse Is Rolled over Hot Spots 69

4.10 Clickable Map with Hot Spot 69

5.1 True-False Quiz Created with PowerPoint 74

5.2 Feedback Provided for First Incorrect Answer 75

5.3 Additional Feedback Shown for Second Incorrect Answer 75

5.4 Feedback for Third Incorrect Answer Directs Learner to Remediation Material 75

5.5 Initial Presentation of Question Using Coursebuilder's Slider Interaction 76

5.6 Result When Learner Slides Bar to Correct Response 76

5.7 Mathematical Quiz Presented in Fill-in-the-Blank Format 77

5.8 Fill-in-the-Blank Foreign Language Vocabulary Quiz 77

5.9 Matching Quiz Created with Hot Potatoes 79

5.10 Drag-and-Drop Quiz Created with Coursebuilder 79

5.11 Game Created with Collaborative Learning Systems Game Template 82

5.12 First Screen of Quia Game Show–Type Game 84

5.13 Quia Screen Showing Hint 84

5.14 Quia Screen Showing Progression to Next Question 85

5.15 Game Board for PowerPoint Game 87

5.16 Question Slide for "Category 1 for $100" 87

5.17 Answer Slide 87

5.18 Example of a Treasure Hunt 90

5.19 Introduction Page for Mad Cow Web Quest 92

5.20 Description of the Assignment 92

5.21 Outline of Process To Be Used 92

5.22 Evaluation Rubric 93

5.23 Conclusion and Suggestions for Additional Resources 93

5.24 References 93

5.25 Example of a Crossword Puzzle Created with Hot Potatoes 94

5.26 Scrambled Jigsaw Puzzle Pieces 95

5.27 Completed Jigsaw Puzzle 95

5.28 Portion of a Simulation Created with PowerPoint 97

6.1 Example of a Blog 104

6.2 Example of a Student Home Page 107

6.3 Quiz Based on Information in Student Home Pages 107

6.4 Assignment for Team Discussion 108

6.5 Team Member Karen's Contribution to the Team Discussion 108

6.6 Team Member Susan's Thoughts on the Team Discussion 109

6.7 Team Member Henry's Additions to the Team Discussion 109

6.8 Red Team's Final Consensus Post 109

6.9 Discussion Thread at End of First Day of Role Play 113

6.10 Example of Storytelling 113

7.1 Typical Training Events in a Career 116

7.2 Where Real Learning Occurs in a Career 116

7.3 Example of "Edit—Find" Command Used to Search a
       Word Document 119

7.4 Sample Warning Letter 121

7.5 Calculator Used in a Farm Supply Store 121

7.6 Performance Support Tool Used by the IRS 122

7.7 Page of Performance Support Tools for Part-Time
       Volunteer Staff 123

10.1 Welcome Page Introducing OTS Course 152

10.2 SkillSoft's Home Page 157

10.3 Washington State Portal Page 158

11.1 Sample Score Report from Quia 168

12.1 Matching e-Learning Approaches to Learner Styles 178

12.2 Home Page of Online Course Hosted by Free
        Online Community 185

12.3 Assignments Created from Free Site's "Files" Page 185

Acknowledgments

IT TAKES THE EFFORTS and support of many to bring a book to publication. I am especially grateful to my Pfeiffer friends: my discoverer and champion, Martin Delahoussaye; acquisitions editor Lisa Shannon; production editor Nina Kreiden; and chronically underthanked senior marketing manager Jeanenne Ray. Thanks also to Will Pearce/ISPI of the Carolinas and Michael McGinnis for planting the first seeds of this project.

I am indebted to the dozens of people willing to let me include quotes, anecdotes, examples, excerpts from interviews, and screen shots from websites. Without exception, folks were happy to help, and, bless their hearts, quick to respond. All of them exemplify the spirit of sharing that I try to espouse.

I owe a great deal to several faculty members (alas, mostly former) of the Training and Development Program at North Carolina State University (NCSU): Darryl McGraw, who in introducing me to the magic of web design quite literally changed my life; also Paula Berardinelli, Diane Chapman, and

Saundra Wall Williams. Many thanks as well to NCSU's Elliott Fisher for the personalized technology demystification tutorials.

Additional warm thanks to the trainers, dear friends and mentors all: head cheerleader Nancy Gustafson, Anne Howard, Rosalie Blowe, Liz Grimes, Nancy Hall, Cindy Thacker, Cindy Epps, and all my other Trainers' Networking Team (TNT) friends. The trick to becoming a good trainer is to spend time with good trainers; I am lucky to have spent so much time with the best.

Last: For me, one of the big surprises of adulthood was the revelation that work can be so meaningful, exciting, and fulfilling. Thanks to the flexibility, encouragement, and support of several employers-friends (or is it the other way 'round?), I spend the bulk of my days in a happy and productive state of flow. Many thanks to Thom Wright, who on hiring me said, "I'll do everything I can to make you successful in this job," and especially the big-hearted and persistent (and tall!) Ann Gillen Cobb, consummate grown-up and really good egg.

                                                                    Jane Bozarth

E-LEARNING SOLUTIONS ON A SHOESTRING

Introduction: Getting the Most from This Resource

ACCORDING TO A SURVEY in the September 2003 issue of *Training* magazine, 39 percent of organizations responding cited cost as a significant reason for limiting the use of e-learning (Hequet, 2003). Despite the myriad benefits e-learning can offer, many organizations—and their employees—are left out in the cold due to the belief that e-learning costs are prohibitively high. Note that the *belief* that costs are high is the limiting factor. That is not necessarily the reality.

What Does e-Learning Typically Cost?

Ballpark estimates for e-learning initiatives tend to look something like this:

- Cost of converting an existing two-hour class to online: $25,000
- Cost of creating a new two-hour online program from scratch: $65,000
- Cost of purchasing a learning management system: $200,000 and up

I am a state government employee. If I went to management asking for $65,000 for a two-hour class, I would be laughed out of the room. I will never have access to that kind of money in this job. Using the techniques and tools described in this book, I have developed and launched, and continue to develop, a statewide e-learning program for essentially the price of my salary, one new computer, and some discounted software. I am proof that having limited resources is no reason to deny employees access to effective, time-saving workplace learning opportunities.

I am on an unending quest to find low-cost alternatives to high-ticket e-learning tools and approaches. And I've been pretty successful. Effective, quality programs can be had for little or no money. The real secret to finding e-learning solutions on a shoestring: be persistent, creative, patient, and, above all, resourceful. Good e-learning programs don't have to be expensive—and a lot of expensive e-learning programs aren't very good!

What Will This Book Do for You?

By the time you finish this book, you will be convinced that for those who are determined and persistent, e-learning is an affordable option. Whether you choose to build your own solutions, purchase off-the-shelf products, or contract for custom services, you will have identified many tools and strategies for cutting costs or even eliminating them altogether. And in addition to offering information about e-learning, this book will give you two more "E"s: by the end of the book, you will feel Encouraged and Empowered.

Who This Book Is For

The intended audience is the training professional trying to move into e-learning with limited funds. Classroom trainers, instructional designers, training managers, and those staffing one-person training operations will find help and encouragement here. This book is especially meant for anyone truly trying to work with very little funding, such as nonprofits, small government agencies, small private companies, and one-stop shops. It is also targeted at those who may not have in-house web developers and graphic artists. I am assuming that you know something about training in general and a little something about e-learning in particular, that you have perhaps taken a few online classes, and maybe you have kept up with information available on the Internet or in professional journals. In short, this book is for anyone who wants to give e-learning a try but thinks it's too expensive and especially those for whom, because of lack of resources, e-learning has been out of the question. I suggest reading the book straight through to get a good overview of the many free and inexpensive possibilities available and then return to chapters as you need them.

What This Book Covers

We first take a look at some general information about e-learning: what it is, why to use it, and what skills and mind-sets are helpful for training professionals who are seeking to obtain e-learning solutions on a shoestring budget. Then we'll look at one of your biggest decisions: Should you buy your e-learning solution or build it yourself?

Chapters Two through Eight cover building free or inexpensive e-learning solutions. Chapter Two invites you to take stock: of inventory, of your learners, and of your real needs (versus your wants). In Chapter Three we'll look at building simple e-learning pages and programs with tools we already have, such as the Microsoft Office products. Chapter Four takes design issues up a notch and offers suggestions for simple low- or no-cost tools for enhancing basic programs. In Chapter Five we'll move on to creating interactivity, from free e-mail games to inexpensive Flash quizzes. Chapter Six examines collaborative activities such as discussion assignments and role plays. Chapter Seven focuses on an idea critical to those working on a tight budget: the fact that e-"learning" isn't always e-"training" and can take the form of very inexpensive, easy-to-create performance support tools. The "doing it yourself" section concludes with Chapter Eight, a look at leveraging resources, expertise, and creating new materials with reuse in mind.

Chapters Nine and Ten move us into the decision to buy, rather than build, solutions, and offer guidelines for saving money when dealing with vendors of both off-the-shelf and custom content. These chapters provide tools for establishing criteria for purchases and offer ideas for negotiating and minimizing expenses. Chapter Eleven discusses the issue of tracking learner data, starting with simple, homemade free methods. For those needing to go beyond basic tracking, there's information on some free learning management systems (LMSs) and, for those needing still more, suggestions for choosing and purchasing a full-blown LMS. Finally, Chapter Twelve is the application chapter, in which we'll take a look at how the tools and ideas presented here can be mixed and matched to create robust e-learning solutions.

For more examples and a chance to look at some working samples of the animated or interactive approaches discussed in this book, be sure to check out this book's companion website (www.bozarthzone.com).

What This Book Does Not Cover

This is not an introduction to technology or a web design primer. Many resources for those pursuits exist, and although I mention quite a few of them, this book is not intended to be a how-to manual. I am interested in showing tools, approaches, and strategies for developing or acquiring e-learning with limited funds. Occasionally I've provided some explanation of how a particular item was created, but in many cases, I instead offer suggestions for ways to research and learn about a certain approach or technique.

Technology Skills

This book is written for the trainer or instructional designer who has used a desktop computer. The assumption is that you have basic computer skills (such as word processing, PowerPoint, and Internet surfing). The information on using what you have in Chapter Three assumes you are working in a Windows environment with access to the Microsoft Office products (Word, PowerPoint, and Excel). Macintosh (Mac) users should be able to relate much of this information to their own situations, and the rest of the chapters largely offer information of a more general nature, relevant to users with either operating system.

If you don't know anything about web design, it's important for you to learn. Developing a little understanding of the technology will make you more competent and confident in dealing with vendors and talking with those responsible for your computer technology, and it will keep you from making expensive mistakes. I hope this book encourages you to give web design a try. Even if it doesn't, though, you'll need to be able to communicate your cost-saving ideas to your designers and vendors; learning to talk a little of the lingo will help. If all the technology just isn't your area, that's okay. After all, you don't need to know how the TV works in order to turn it on. But you probably know enough about TVs to buy one without getting ripped off.

Hardware and Software

This book assumes that if you will be building any solutions in-house, you have access to a telephone and a computer with Windows 98 or better; Microsoft Office products, particularly Word and PowerPoint, and some experience using them; e-mail; and Internet access.

Special Things to Watch For

Free. This word in bold type appears throughout the book to draw attention to particular products and to serve as a frequent reminder of the many tools and options available entirely for free. In some cases, they are things you may not be aware of; in others, they are free e-learning tools we perhaps take for granted and therefore underuse, such as e-mail.

The scorecard boxes reveal actual costs of creating a given product or example. Where appropriate, I've included side-by-side comparisons of costs of homemade versus store-bought solutions.

SCORECARD

Cost of outsourcing creation of custom-designed 5-minute Flash movie with animated text and audio: $500

Cost of creating similar product with PowerPoint: $0

Sometimes finding a free or inexpensive solution is just knowing where to look. The binoculars icon denotes suggested phrases for searching the web. I like the Google search engine (http://www.google.com), but others will give you different results. Try also http://www.msn.com, http://www.yahoo.com, and http://www.lycos.com. For images and sounds, give http://www.altavista.com a try. One of the best free tools of all is the Internet itself. If you are not already a strong web searcher, now is a good time to expand your skills.

The book concludes with a references list, which gives citation information for sources directly quoted or data referenced, and a resources list of many of the web sites, products, and other materials mentioned throughout this book.

The Best Thing You Can Do

The best way to learn this material is to try it out. Take as many free online courses as you can. Visit the websites I mention, and try the searches I recommend. Take advantage of demo offers, trial periods, and pilot programs. Play online games; join online communities for trainers, e-learning developers, and web designers. Develop the habit of looking at products and asking, "How did they do that? Can I do that? Is there a cheaper way to do that?" Learning to view products with a developer's eye will help you hone your skills at creating or purchasing solutions.

Disclaimer

This book references a number of websites and particular products. There is always danger here, particularly when talking about web technologies: site addresses change, companies merge and change hands, and products disappear. I have tried as much as possible to stick with sites likely to be around for a long time, such as www.microsoft.com. Too, my mention of particular products should not be taken to mean that similar offerings are not good. Many products will, for instance, allow you to create Flash games as described in Chapter Five. I've presented examples from two vendors that have good track records, whose games I have used, and that provide extensive support and training for their products.

Another consideration in mentioning products is cost. An early reader of the manuscript for this book, commenting on one of the techniques described, said, "You could do this more quickly with Product X." That's true, but Product X costs nearly six thousand dollars (and has a very long learning curve). In the spirit of working on a shoestring, I have tried for the most part to limit discussion of specific products to those ranging in price from free to no more than $500.

E-learning technologies are constantly emerging and evolving. Keep looking for new products, and experiment as much as you can. And please, share what you learn, what you create, and what you know.

e-Learning
Some Basics

T HE FACT THAT E-LEARNING *can* be done cheaply does not always mean it *should* be done cheaply—or, in fact, always done at all. E-learning is a great approach when used thoughtfully and for the right reasons. But I've seen it used badly and seen costs cut to the point of rendering the final product useless. This chapter provides some basics about the uses of e-learning, its benefits, and the decision to move online. We'll also look at considerations when working on a shoestring budget, including the crucial issue of avoiding costly mistakes. Finally, we'll take a look at one of your biggest decisions: whether to buy your solution or build it yourself.

What Is e-Learning?

E-learning has many definitions and takes many forms. My definition—as someone working with very limited funds—is broader than most others. I think of it as anything designed to improve work performance delivered by any electronic means. So my terms would regard e-learning as any training or performance support delivered with any mechanism provided by computer: on the web, through a CD or DVD, or by performance support tools, like checklists and descriptions of processes, available electronically. It can be a pre- or postclassroom activity involving online chat or e-mail discussion; it can be a blended event, in which cognitive information is offered online with an accompanying follow-up group workshop; it can be a relationship with a virtual mentor or community of practice. Basically, I think of e-learning as anything that solves a training or performance problem through the use of computer technologies.

Why Use e-Learning?

E-learning offers many advantages. It provides for just-in-time training; a new supervisor needing to hone her delegation skills needn't wait until the live class is offered again. It can save travel costs, because employees don't have to go to a remote site (which is inconvenient for them as well). It can reduce other costs associated with training, such as trainer salaries, classroom rentals, equipment purchases, and printing expenses. It can reduce the costs and inconvenience associated with having employees away from work. It can ensure consistency in delivery; everyone gets the same message every time. Finally, good e-learning gives the learner some control over when and where to take the program, in choosing when to take breaks (or not), and in deciding which elements of the training are relevant. Used appropriately, e-learning is not only "just-in-time" but also "just-for-me."

But e-learning, one way or another, *is* expensive. Even "free" approaches incur costs in terms of time and energy. When deciding whether e-learning is right for your organization, give some thought to the items in Table 1.1 and check off those that describe your situation. If more than half of them fit, an online training approach is appropriate.

TABLE 1.1. E-LEARNING OR CLASSROOM DECISION CRITERIA

Source: Terrell Perry, Coastal Training Technologies Corporation
(http://coastal.com). Used with permission.

Criterion	Describes My Situation
Organization seeks to reduce worker time spent away from work in training	
Organization/topic demands consistency in delivery	
Content is stable or can be changed in predictable, manageable amounts	
Content is largely cognitive or informational in nature	
Target audience is large or widely scattered	
Target audience has diverse skills or varied proficiency levels	
Target audience has wide-ranging learning styles	
Content is dangerous to perform or requires equipment that is costly to take out of service, scarce, or sensitive	
Qualified trainers are scarce or unavailable or hard to schedule	
Workers find it difficult to take time from work to attend training	

Moving from Classroom to Online

In thinking about using e-learning, consider the activities and approaches that typically make up the classroom experience:

- Lecture

- Lecture and PowerPoint shows

- Stories, anecdotes, and metaphors

- Asking and answering questions

- Videos

- Music

- Quizzes, tests, assessments, certifications, and feedback

- Case studies

- Role plays

- Group activities

- Self-disclosure exercises, in which learners share something about themselves

- Reflection activities, such as journal-writing, in which learners are asked to reflect on course material or personal experiences

- Having the learner demonstrate a skill

- Pre- and postwork

- Working with equipment, such as in a computer lab

- Readings

- Meetings outside class

All of these things can be done online, most as well as, and some better than, in the classroom. Throughout this book, we'll look at low-cost ways of replicating many of these activities and examine some new ones as well.

Some New Ways of Thinking

This book assumes that you have some experience with classroom training and workplace learning. You already know the basics of engaging an audience, creating interesting activities, and gearing instruction toward desired outcomes. You know how to develop a lesson plan, choose visuals, and facilitate group interactions. And you know a lot about your learners: their reading levels, their work schedules, and their general attitude toward training. As you prepare to move toward e-learning, particularly if you're working on a shoestring budget, it's important to develop manageable expectations and anticipate some adjustments to your knowledge base.

For one thing, you will need to be realistic about the size of your e-learning initiative. If you are a small, or poor, or one-person training shop, your first move into e-learning may be as simple as just putting a manual online.

Then you might add a homemade PowerPoint show, gradually develop a roster of courses, and eventually find the need to look seriously at a robust learning management system (LMS).

You may also discover that in some cases, it makes more sense to blend your e-learning programs by combining online materials with classroom activities. Many e-learning programs use the web to supply learners with pre- or postclassroom work, with supplemental case studies, or with manuals, forms, and other documents that are cumbersome to copy, bind, and hand out. Time in the classroom can then be spent on action learning activities such as role plays and hands-on practice rather than on lecture or presentation of material.

Another adjustment for those experienced with classroom training is the idea of size or length of training programs. Effective e-learning typically consists of small chunks or nuggets of information and instruction. Online, there are no three-full-day courses: as a rule of thumb, fifteen to twenty-five minutes of asynchronous training (with the learner working alone at a computer) at a stretch is about all a learner can remain alert for. Although this may present a change for you, learning to chunk information brings a big advantage for those working with limited funds: small pieces of instruction are much easier to create, reuse, recycle, and repurpose, which can help enormously in saving costs.

Although much of your classroom experience will transfer to the online training environment, the move to e-learning will require you to develop some new skills. Do-it-yourself approaches may require developing knowledge of web design or instructional planning. Buying solutions and negotiating for deals will demand that you educate yourself about products and technologies. I hope you see this as a challenging opportunity and find it an enjoyable and satisfying way to stretch and grow. There is a bonus to this as well: learning some tech talk will go a long way toward helping you build a relationship with your information technology (IT) or other computer support staff or outside designers and developers. You'll have a better understanding of what you're asking them to do—like whether it's a five-minute or five-day task—and you'll be better able to articulate what you want. Perhaps they, in turn, will be willing to learn a little more about training delivery and instructional design.

Finally, realize that while good e-learning solutions can be had on limited resources, there are going to be some trade-offs. Doing things cheaply sometimes means they won't be elegant. Although you don't want to end up with shoddy or poorly designed work, neither will you always be able to obtain top-of-the-line animation or custom multimedia. I'm not suggesting that you should launch amateurish programs, but if I were a learner with the choice between playing a homemade PowerPoint game or driving three hours to sit in a classroom and be presented with the same material, I'd take the Power-Point game. You will need to make some decisions about acceptable quality and must-have versus nice-to-have features and capabilities. Keep in mind that many expensive e-learning products come with lots of glitter, bells, and whistles but nevertheless fail in their intent to teach. Whatever resources you do have, try to invest them in the things that matter. Though it's true that learners can be seduced by pretty pages and gimmicky animations, I'd argue they care more about a quality learning experience—and feeling that their time was used well—than in using a flashy, expensive product that wasted their time.

Avoiding Costly Mistakes

As you work to develop e-learning solutions, it's important to act carefully and thoughtfully. If it's any consolation, the fact that you have limited resources may actually work in your favor. Having little money can save you from the expensive e-learning missteps some organizations have made:

- The large government entity that estimated first-year use at 30,000 and purchased licenses accordingly. Actual first-year use: 2,000.

- The agency that bought a product unaware that running it would require the purchase of another product.

- The school that bought an authoring program so complex that no one could ever figure it out.

- The training unit that purchased an LMS that didn't fit with any of the organization's other data systems.

- The midwestern state government system with such poor internal communication that at one point, forty different agencies had negotiated forty different contracts—with the same e-learning vendor.

- The organization that spent half its e-learning budget on expensive game creation software: only one person can run it, and employees are already bored with the games.

This book is meant to help you leverage your resources, avoid expensive mistakes, and craft or purchase your own good solutions without breaking your bank. Take your time and think through what you really want to accomplish. Also, seek out other resources and experts to help you learn about e-learning. The more educated you are as a consumer, the less likely you'll fall into one of the traps listed above.

The Case of the Early Adopter

In the early 1960s, Emmett Rogers (1995) introduced his theory of diffusion of innovations, outlining the ways in which people tend to adopt technology. A handful of us are what Rogers calls "early adopters." You probably know the type: they buy the new gadget or product the day it's introduced, when it's huge and complicated, with many bugs still needing to be worked out. Of course, the world needs early adopters; without them, no new piece of technology would ever get off the ground. But it helps to have less-early adopter types around to temper things.

A training colleague, formerly a middle school teacher, tells this story. In the late 1970s, the school's principal returned from a conference enamored of a new technology he called the "VRC." (That is not a typo. He thought it was "VRC," not "VCR.") At the next faculty meeting, the principal announced that the VRC was the "wave of the future" that would "change classroom instruction forever." He then said he'd spent more than half of the next year's budget on beta-format video cameras and other equipment. His plan was to tape his teachers delivering their "best lessons" (fractions, geography, and so forth), which middle school students would then be eager to watch at their leisure.

The result: unwatched videos, wasted time, and the loss of half the annual budget.

Using e-Learning: Buy Off-the-Shelf or Build It Yourself?

Once you've decided that e-learning is right for your situation, you have a big decision to make: Will you build a custom solution, or will you buy a ready-made off-the-shelf (OTS) product? And if you decide you need a custom solution, will you build it yourself or hire an outside contractor to do the work? Although those with scarce resources say hiring a contractor or purchasing an OTS product is out of the question, assess the real cost of doing the work yourself: your time and salary, including whether you'll have to learn a new piece of software from scratch. Consider too the time and salary of coworkers who may need to be involved. If there's any chance at all of finding money, you may want to try to make a case for outsourcing the development or purchasing an OTS program.

In making this decision, consider how many people will use the product. It doesn't make sense to spend two hundred person-hours creating an online program that will be used by only fifteen people. Unless the information is proprietary and absolutely requires company-specific language or graphics *and* will be used by more than five hundred learners, then using an off-the-shelf product will likely be your truly less expensive choice. Figure 1.1 presents a flowchart of the buy-versus-build decision.

You'll notice that an alternative to buying an OTS product outright is customizing one. This can be done not only by the vendor reworking the product (an expensive proposition) but also through providing your own introductory, supplementary, or concluding content. Think of this as adding on to, rather than renovating, the OTS program. We'll look at this further in Chapter Ten with an example of a how a simple clarifying "welcome" page made it possible to use a great off-the-shelf product at minimal cost.

Another option is that it's possible to obtain an OTS solution entirely for **free.** For instance, there are dozens of free web tutorials on common computer applications, such as adding narration to PowerPoint or creating spreadsheets in Excel. One of these may very well solve your problem. (There may

FIGURE 1.1. BUY-VERSUS-BUILD FLOWCHART

Source: Copyright © January 2002 from Learning Circuits by Laura Francis. Reprinted with permission of the American Society for Training and Development.

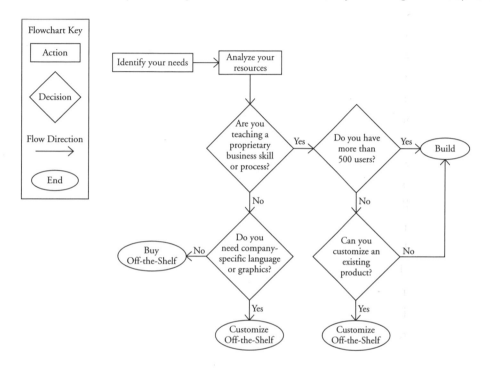

even be a more local solution for you. Many people don't realize that Windows XP installs with built-in animated, narrated tutorials for many of the functions of Microsoft Office products.) You may need to do some homework first—the tutorials vary widely in quality—but searching the web for "Excel spreadsheet tutorial" or "adding narration to MS PowerPoint" might give you a no-cost ready-made solution.

Another issue to consider is your vision. What do you want your e-learning program to look like next year? In two years? Do you want a few quick modules to cover your organization's mandatory topics, a single online orientation program for new employees, or a robust catalogue with a thousand courses? Factor these considerations into your buy-versus-build decision too.

Summary

Good e-learning has the potential to change the face of workplace performance improvement. Apart from the many cost savings are the opportunities to make training more accessible and useful to learners. Another plus is that once you've demonstrated some small successes with your thrifty approach to e-learning, your managers and budget staff might be more willing to start talking about money for additional projects. In Chapter Two, we'll look at getting started in building e-learning solutions by taking stock of the assets you already have.

Part One

Doing It Yourself

Getting Started with Doing It Yourself

THE DECISION TO BUILD can be both exhilarating and daunting. My best advice, especially when you're starting out, is to take your time and give some real thought to what you want to do. The potential to waste money is enormous. You don't want to misstep and buy something you don't need or, worse, something you already have. This chapter will help you evaluate your haves, wants, and needs.

Taking Inventory: You Probably Have More Than You Think

Before you rush out to buy anything, take a good look at what you have, or at least what you can get your hands on. Be creative and be specific—and ask. I once started a new job and, worried about losing my files, asked for a $200 external hard drive. Weeks later I discovered all employees had private space on the organization's network drive. That $200 could have bought a digital camera, thousands of blank CDs, or captioning software. It was an expensive lesson to learn.

When taking inventory, be sure to venture outside your own office: someone down the hall may own a digital video camera or CD burner. Using Table 2.1, put a check mark in the boxes next to things you own and plus signs next to things you believe you might have access to.

TABLE 2.1. INVENTORY CHECKLIST

	Hardware		Software
	Computer		Word processing
	CD/DVD burner		PowerPoint
	Scanner		Spreadsheet
	Extra data storage		MS Photo Editor
	Microphone		MS Paint
	Headset		HTML editing software (FrontPage, Dreamweaver)
	Video capture card or video capture device		Course authoring software (Toolbook, Authorware)
	Digital camera		Adobe Acrobat
	Digital video camera		E-mail
	Server on which to run e-learning or contract with web hosting service		Advanced graphics editing program: Fireworks, Photoshop, Paintshop
	Telephone		Movie editing program
	Web camera		Animation editor (Flash)
	Sound card and speakers		Academic platform: BlackBoard, WebCT
	Color printer		Screen capture software
			Web conferencing tool: for example, NetMeeting or Centra
			CD creation software

In addition to the material resources available, take stock of the people around you. Do you have within reach?

- Someone who knows web design? If not, who will learn it?
- Instructional designers and training staff in-house?
- A graphic artist? If not, then someone who can draw? If not even that, then someone who has an eye for color and design?
- Technical and administrative support?
- Coworkers or friends with acting skills? Someone with a good voice for narration?

A final note about taking inventory: don't forget about the vast training materials you probably already own. Class handouts, graphics in overhead transparencies, and even old videotapes can be repurposed for e-learning applications.

What Else Should You Have?

While I do encourage you to use what's at your disposal, you will want to get your hands on a few basics in order to create many from-scratch e-learning solutions. If you don't have these already, try to get access to them (note that "access to" doesn't necessarily mean "buy"):

- A computer with at least Windows 98, but better with Windows XP. You'll need plenty of memory too, as graphics, especially animation and video, take up big amounts of space. Even PowerPoint files can be huge. You'll also want a CD-ROM drive. If you're sure you'll be doing a lot of in-house development and think you might be using sophisticated graphics like video, try to get the best machine you can afford. (The rule of thumb is that the development computer will cost about double the price of the average user's computer.) The one thing we did splurge on is my top-of-the-line computer. It's very fast and holds huge amounts of information, so I can do things like edit video with no worries. Even though I believe in "cheap," I do have a salary, and my time spent dealing with a slow or temperamental computer would cost my agency more in the long run than just buying a good computer. I got along fine for several years, though, with a less sophisticated machine, so don't feel discouraged if there's no money in your budget now for something better. Factor in the sophistication of the products you'll be developing and the reality of your budget. Too, depending on your needs, leasing the equipment might be a better choice for you.

- Fast Internet access—anything but dial-up (T-1 line, DSL)
- A microphone, which typically costs less than $20

User Considerations

If this is your organization's first foray into the world of e-learning, you will need to scan the technology situation of your learners before creating any solutions:

- Does your organization have standard equipment?
- Does everyone have access to a computer?
- Do you have people located in field offices, in the hinterlands, or working primarily from their cars? Are their machines as good as the ones at your headquarters? Do they have the same Internet access as you?

Table 2.2 will help you assess what technology is available to your users.

TABLE 2.2. TECHNOLOGY ASSESSMENT

Item		Notes
Computer		
Own computer		
Access to computer		
Operating system		
Apple		
Windows XP		

TABLE 2.2. TECHNOLOGY ASSESSMENT *(continued)*

Item		Notes
Operating system		
Windows 2000		
Windows 98		
Windows other		
Hardware		
Speakers		
Printer		
CD drive		
Software and plug-ins		
PowerPoint		
Flash player		
Windows Media player		
QuickTime player		
Text-to-speech engine enabled		
Internet		
Dial-up access		
T-1 lines		
DSL		
Other		
Security		
Filters to block access to sites or content?		
Firewall issues that prevent access to common web tools such as chat, instant messaging, or web conferencing?		
Cookies enabled?		

A rule of thumb is to design for the 75 percent; that is, if 75 percent of your users have sound cards and speakers, then you can use audio. Have a plan, though, for making sure the program is somehow accessible (for instance, arrange for use of someone else's machine) to users who do not have the technology. Avoid the temptation to design for the lowest common denominator (LCD). If developing for your LCD would result in programs that are nothing but text on a screen, you will lose learners who are used to more sophisticated technology and likely fail to engage even those with the LCD machines.

Some organizations hesitate to implement e-learning because all employees don't have their own good computers—or even their own machines. In most cases, users just need occasional computer access. In fact, one of the biggest obstacles for e-learners is the problem of interruptions. Consider, for example, the situation of the receptionist trying to complete a twenty-minute online customer service program at her desk while greeting office visitors and answering the phone. The constant interruptions will be frustrating and prove a serious obstacle to learning. It might be better to arrange for such a learner to use a computer in another office or other quiet private space.

In addition to assessing the equipment available, consider the technology skills of your users. It's tempting to assume that everyone by now has basic computer skills, but it's better to be safe than sorry. Many workers use their computers as nothing more than expensive typewriters. Do your learners know how to attach a Word document and e-mail it to you? How to browse for a file? What *right-click* means? Think about how sophisticated your learners are, keep this in mind when you're designing, and be prepared to provide skills training if necessary.

Lesson Learned

Before you invest in e-learning, built, bought, or otherwise, get a realistic assessment of the situation of your users. I once worked with an organization whose training manager requested the design of an online course for her staff. She assumed (and I assumed she knew what she was talking about) that everyone involved had the same technology as she. She was housed at headquarters. I found out—too late—that the field staff did not have the Flash player and were not allowed to install it, and that the only real technical support existed in the head-quarters building. And due to the confidential nature of the business, the orga-nization had significant security issues: extensive firewalls and filters wreaked havoc with attempts to deliver the online product. There were also nightmarish bandwidth issues. Though most of the course was homemade, it was incredibly expensive in terms of wasted time.

Before developing a product, do a technology and skills scan, talk to more than one person, and be sure to check the field offices.

Want versus Need: What Will Meet Your Objectives?

Although it is tempting to want slick, impressive multimedia for every pro-gram, many times it is more technology than needed to meet the learn-ing objectives. For example, suppose you are responsible for orienting new health care technician staff. They provide some simple medical tasks, like taking temperatures and pulses. One of the training performance objectives is that the technicians will distinguish a normal heartbeat from an abnor-mal one.

Figure 2.1 shows an excellent tutorial on heart sounds. It's a simulation designed for medical students that provides patient history, offers branching decisions, teaches how to differentiate first from second heart sounds, and shows an animated pulse at the throat. The product is meant to, and succeeds at, teaching fine differentiation among assorted heart sounds. It's very advanced, very good, and very expensive to build (it is also available for you to view, for **free**, from Blaufuss Multimedia; see http://www.blaufuss.org/tutorial/).

FIGURE 2.1. SOPHISTICATED MULTIMEDIA HEART SOUNDS TUTORIAL

Source: Used with permission of Blaufuss Multimedia (www.blaufuss.org).

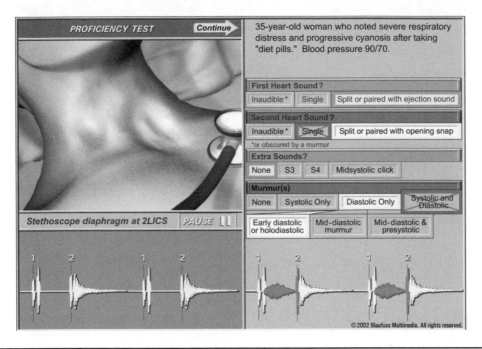

Do you want this? Perhaps. But do you need this to meet your learning objectives? Probably not. If learners need only to make basic differentiation, they could listen to a side-by-side comparison of sounds, as illustrated in Figure 2.2. These are embedded in a PowerPoint slide. The cost? $0. And this basic approach could be enhanced by the addition of graphics, as shown in Figure 2.3. The cost? $0.

Neither solution is elegant, but each will get the job done. In working on a shoestring budget it's vital to decide what you really must have and then choose the tools and approaches that will get you there.

FIGURE 2.2. CLICKABLE HEART SOUNDS

Normal mitral valve   Stenosed mitral valve

**Click on the horns to hear the difference between a
normal and a stenosed valve.**

FIGURE 2.3. ILLUSTRATED CLICKABLE HEART SOUNDS

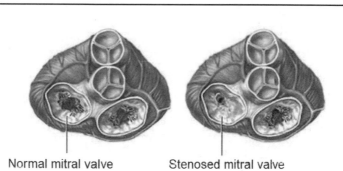

Normal mitral valve   Stenosed mitral valve

**Click on the pictures to hear the difference between a
normal and a stenosed valve.**

Sale!

Pay attention to the Sunday newspaper inserts from office supply, computer, and electronics stores. By watching for sales, using coupons, and mailing in certificates for rebates I have acquired:

- Scanner: $9.99

- 5 power strips: $0

- USB mouse: $0

- 12 sets of computer speakers: $9

- USB Flash drive: $6.99

- 1,000 blank CDs: $0

- 600 CD jewel cases: $0

- 10 microphones: $0

- CD labeler: $9.99

- Color printer with ink cartridge and cable: $39.99

Summary

Before spending any money on anything, determine what you really need. Then go back and take stock of what you already have, which is likely much more than you realize. Clarifying your needs, capabilities, and the situation of your learners will help you make good decisions about development and purchases. In the next chapter, we'll look at building basic programs with the resources you already have.

Building Simple Pages and Programs

IF YOU ARE NEW TO THE idea of creating from-scratch web pages, you may be surprised to learn that it is not necessarily an expensive undertaking. You can build basic e-learning programs with good graphics and simple interactions using tools you already have, such as the Microsoft (MS) Office programs and e-mail. In this chapter, we'll look at some of the possibilities for building basic e-learning with these products and end with a discussion of making the move to additional development tools.

In approaching e-learning on a shoestring, especially of the do-it-yourself variety, try to start small. Think about your areas of greatest need and likely successes. Consider this, from www.e-learningcentreuk.com's director Jane Knight: "The emphasis [should be] on small, manageable pieces of content, which can be quickly and easily created, and which meet a short-term need. Such solutions do not need to be overengineered and designed."

In approaching this information, realize that the material in this and several of the following chapters is meant to help you understand, and feel encouraged about, the many possibilities for creating your own inexpensive e-learning solutions. For help with the how-to's of web design and graphics, try starting with Thomas Toth's *Technology for Trainers* (2003), Lisa Lopuck's *Web Design for Dummies* (2001), and Bud Smith and Arthur Bebank's *Creating Web Pages for Dummies* (2004). Online resources include Microsoft's excellent Office product support site (http://office.microsoft.com) and its support site for education (http://www.microsoft.com/Education/Default.aspx). If you are fortunate enough to have an in-house web developer or graphics designer, try as much as possible to draw on that resource as well.

Using What You Already Have: MS Office Products and MS Paint

Products such as MS PowerPoint, Word, Paint, and even Excel and Access can be used for creating or supporting e-learning.

MS PowerPoint

It seems safe to assume that if you're already involved in training, you probably know something about using PowerPoint. For those just beginning to build e-learning programs, PowerPoint is a good place to start and an excellent way to build confidence for moving to more advanced web design. You may even find that it's all you really need: e-learning consultants Clive Shepard (http://fastrack-consulting.co.uk) and Josh Bersin (http://www.bersin.com) both report that as much as half of all workplace e-learning programs are developed with PowerPoint. There are those who would have you believe that web pages with animated graphics, moving text, sound effects, and interactivity can be created only by expensive Flash (Macromedia's animation creation/editing software) designers. But it's often possible to create similar effects with PowerPoint, so for those starting out, those working from a very limited budget, or those in need of a quick solution, PowerPoint can be a wonderful tool. An added benefit is that if e-learning is new to your users, PowerPoint-based programs will also probably be sophisticated enough for them, at least to start.

A word of caution: a distressing but increasingly common occurrence is the poorly designed classroom PowerPoint show uploaded to the web and renamed "e-learning." As trainers, it's important for us to fight this trend. E-learning programs, regardless of cost, still need to provide the basics of good training: well-defined performance objectives and outcomes, the opportunity for interactivity and practice, support for the learner, and use of sound instructional design principles.

Case Study: A Shoestring Solution Created with PowerPoint

The problem: all employees had received initial required training on the Americans with Disabilities Act (ADA) in 2002. However, subsequent U.S. Supreme Court decisions affected interpretation of the act, and this information needed to be delivered to staff very quickly. Rather than call all the employees back to the classroom, a short update program was developed entirely in PowerPoint and included animated text effects, animated graphics, a quiz, and narration. The course was developed in less than a week and delivered to all employees within ten working days. Cost: $0.

FIGURE 3.1. COMPONENTS OF A TYPICAL COURSE CREATED IN POWERPOINT

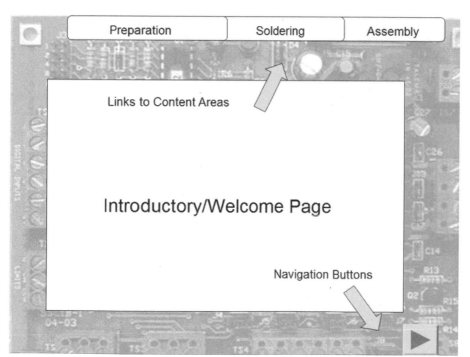

PowerPoint Tools. The use of PowerPoint in e-learning ranges from insertion of a simple animation into a web page to the delivery of entire courses online. A course created in PowerPoint would typically include the items shown on the sample title slide in Figure 3.1. Creating the program involves use of the tools and strategies described below.

Hyperlinking. For basic navigation, PowerPoint lets the learner advance to the next slide by clicking the space bar or Enter key. The designer can also insert customizable buttons, as shown in Figure 3.2. These buttons allow the designer to create more elaborate navigation because they can be set to link to any other slide, file, or even external site and can provide the learner with visual cues for moving through the program. To access the buttons, click "Slide Show" and then "Action Buttons."

FIGURE 3.2. POWERPOINT ACTION BUTTONS

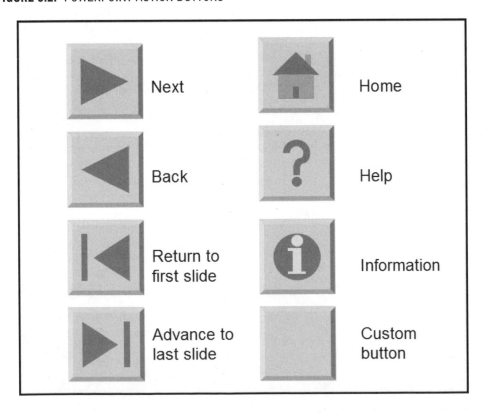

PowerPoint also allows much more sophisticated navigation. The designer can create hyperlinks from text boxes, graphics, and other elements placed on a slide. These will take the learner from this selected *hot spot* or *hot object* (or whole slide) to another slide within the same show, another PowerPoint show, a website, or a document such as a Word or PDF file. A hyperlink to an e-mail address will, when clicked, open an already-addressed e-mail window on the learner's computer screen.

Hyperlinks are inserted by clicking to highlight the object to be linked, then choosing "Insert—Hyperlink" and selecting the link's destination. Figure 3.3 shows the example of a text box hyperlinked to another slide. When viewed in slide show mode, clicking on the word *Temperatures* will take the learner directly to the "temperatures" slide.

FIGURE 3.3. TEXT BOX PROGRAMMED TO HYPERLINK TO ANOTHER SLIDE

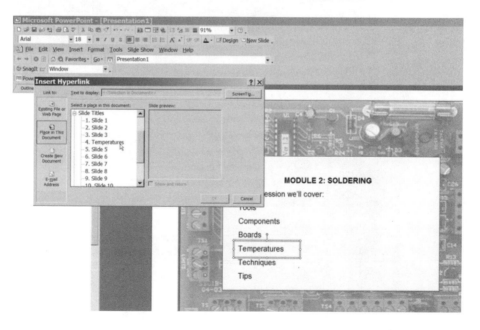

Animations. Each new release of PowerPoint comes with more choices for animations, such as flying text, dissolving objects, and spinning images. In e-learning programs, use of animation often includes actions like moving

chart elements (in which, for instance, the bars on a graph appear to grow taller), progressively revealed lines of text, and illustrations of the sequence of steps in a process. (Note: the examples below were created with PowerPoint 2000. Though different versions of PowerPoint have somewhat different visual elements, the commands for creating effects are the same.) Figure 3.4 shows how to program an animation: choose the object and then "Slide Show— Custom Animation" from the drop-down menu. Figure 3.5 shows selecting an animation from the drop-down menu. When the soldering iron is viewed in slide show mode, it zooms in from the center of the screen.

FIGURE 3.4. PROGRAMMING AN ANIMATION

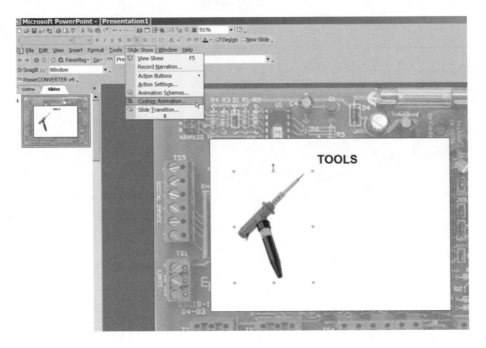

In addition to allowing the designer to choose the order and timing of animations, PowerPoint provides a number of preset animated transitions between slides ("Slide Show—Slide Transition"). Working examples and instructions for creating several PowerPoint animations are provided at http://www.bozarthzone.com.

FIGURE 3.5. SELECTING AN ANIMATION FROM THE DROP-DOWN MENU

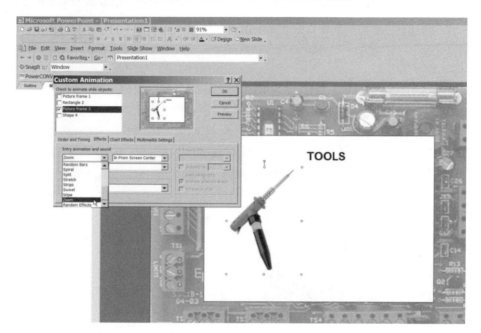

Sound Effects and Narration. PowerPoint comes with an assortment of sound effects: doorbells, barking dogs, music clips, and more. These are easy to use: insert them as you would a photo or piece of clip art (using either "Insert— Movies and Sounds" or the clip art icon on the drawing toolbar).

Narration is easily done with a computer microphone. These range in price from about $4 to $20. A good-quality headset-style microphone both reduces outside noise and allows you to have your hands free for working with your computer keyboard and handling your notes, but a cheaper mic will work too. To record narration, click "Slide Show—Record Narration," and follow the instructions. Figures 3.6 and 3.7 illustrate the process. It really is just click-and-go, but you might also want to search the web for additional tips and tutorials on adding sound to slide shows. Also, prior to recording narration, you'll be prompted to choose the sound quality (the better the quality, the bigger the file) and check the microphone level.

FIGURE 3.6. RECORDING NARRATION BY CLICKING "SLIDE SHOW—RECORD NARRATION"

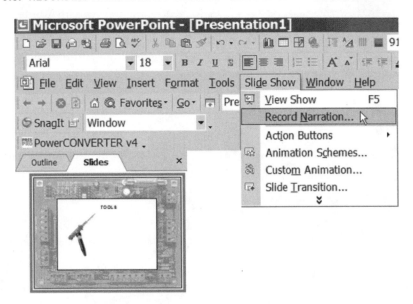

FIGURE 3.7. SELECTING QUALITY OF RECORDING

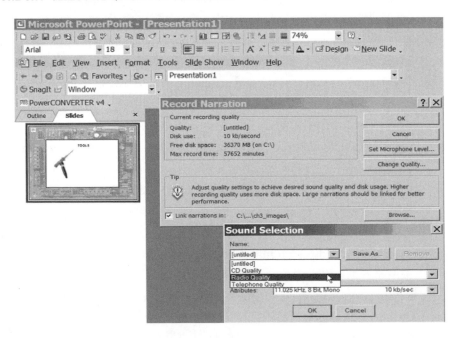

All you really need to get started is access to a microphone, a computer, and PowerPoint. Also, many people don't realize they already own a simple sound editing device: the Sound Recorder that comes with Windows. Click "Start—Programs—Accessories—Entertainment—Sound Recorder" to access this. Should you find you need more sophisticated audio capability, sound editing software can be had for as little as $60.

Video. It is similarly easy to add video clips to PowerPoint shows ("Insert—Movies and Sounds"), but this will dramatically increase the file size. Depending on your circumstances, such as your company's intranet's bandwidth limitations, you may need to be creative when using video. For instance, you could link from your PowerPoint show to a video clip stored as a smaller Flash file elsewhere on your server or use one of the conversion products discussed below in "Publishing PowerPoint to the Web" to reduce the file size.

SCORECARD

Cost: Homemade PowerPoint versus Custom Flash

Cost of outsourcing the creation of a custom-designed five-minute Flash movie with animated text and audio: $500

Cost of creating a similar product with PowerPoint: $0

Publishing PowerPoint to the Web. In providing PowerPoint courses to learners, there are several options. A consideration in using PowerPoint for developing e-learning is file size. PowerPoint slide shows, particularly those with many animations and additions such as narration and music, are enormous. Although it is possible to deliver shows over the web in their original form, this can cause problems for the person loading the files to the server, the learner trying to view the slides, and the organization concerned with bandwidth. A popular solution is the use of a software add-on that converts PowerPoint files to smaller files such as Flash. (The Flash player is available for **free** download from http://www.macromedia.com and comes already installed on most new computers.)

There are dozens of conversion products available: most begin at around $300, though it's not unusual to find them on sale. Many vendors offer free trial periods as well, so it's possible to try them out before buying. Be aware that different products vary in which—or how well—animations and other features convert, so taking advantage of trial periods will help you choose the product that best suits your needs. Some include additional capabilities, such as allowing the insertion of talking-head video of the narrator, the creation of auto-run executable files for CD-ROM or DVD versions of the Power-Point shows, or the delivery of programs embedded in e-mail. Try a web search for "PowerPoint converter" to get a look at the different products that exist. Many of the sites include galleries of sample programs and can be a good source of ideas for the designer working with PowerPoint.

If you choose not to use a conversion product, you'll need to save the program by clicking "File—Save As Web Page—Publish." When launched, the program will appear with a frame containing the program outline, a frame containing the slide, navigation controls, and controls that allow the learner to close the frames and view the program as a full screen presentation. Although the frame view reduces the slide size, some designers take advantage of a special characteristic provided by PowerPoint's "Save As Web Page" command: the appearance in the online product of text typed into the original presentation as speaker notes. Figure 3.8 shows the screen as it will appear when viewed by learners. To view the show saved as a web page, learners will either need PowerPoint on their machines or will need to download the **free** PowerPoint viewer from http://www.Microsoft.com.

Be creative and learn as much as you can about using PowerPoint; don't limit yourself to bulleted lists on a screen. Try to think less in terms of "moving PowerPoint shows to the web" and more in terms of using PowerPoint to replicate features from higher-end (such as Flash) online training programs. PowerPoint can be used to develop everything from straight text–based content to animated demos of policy practices to, as we'll see in Chapter Five, quiz-show–style games and simulations with branching decision making. Given its many features, you may find that PowerPoint solves most of your

FIGURE 3.8. POWERPOINT SHOW SAVED AS A WEB PAGE

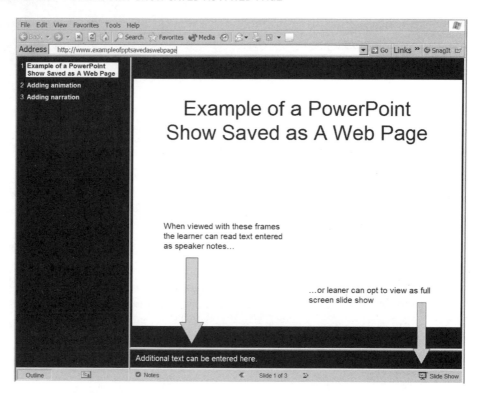

e-learning problems. To learn more about making full use of PowerPoint's capabilities try searching for "PowerPoint animation tutorial" and "using hyperlinking in PowerPoint." Tutorials for creating interesting animations and text effects are also available at http://www.bozarthzone.com.

A final word on PowerPoint: it's a great tool for creating a rough draft or "storyboard" of your e-learning project. Even if you eventually use another tool for creating your final programs, PowerPoint provides a quick, easy way of creating sample pages/screens and trying different layouts for text and images.

Microsoft Word

It's also possible to create web pages from MS Word. Word's excellent Web Page Wizard tool (found under "File—New—New From Template—General Templates") provides help, sets up layout and styles, and creates links among pages. Figure 3.9 shows an example of a typical page layout template provided by Word's Web Page Wizard. To create a new page, the developer types new words over the existing text and inserts new images. Figures 3.10 and 3.11 show part of an e-learning course developed with the MS Word Web Page Wizard template shown in Figure 3.9.

FIGURE 3.9. EXAMPLE OF A WORD WEB PAGE WIZARD LAYOUT TEMPLATE

TYPE THE MAIN HEADING HERE	
Section 1 Part 1 Part 2 Part 3	Section 1 Heading Move cursor to beginning of line and start typing. Enter text wherever you like. Enter text wherever you like. Enter text wherever you like.
Section 2 Part 1 Part 2 Part 3	Section 2 Heading Enter text wherever you like. Enter text wherever you like. Enter text wherever you like. Enter text wherever you like.
Section 3 Part 1 Part 2 Part 3	Section 3 Heading Enter text wherever you like. Enter text wherever you like. Enter text wherever you like. Enter text wherever you like.
INSERT IMAGE HERE INSERT CAPTION HERE	

Word's "Insert—Hyperlink" command allows you to create navigation that includes linking from a web page created in Word to other pages, other programs, and other websites, or insert a link to an e-mail address. For

FIGURE 3.10. COURSE MAIN PAGE CREATED WITH WORD WEB PAGE WIZARD TEMPLATE

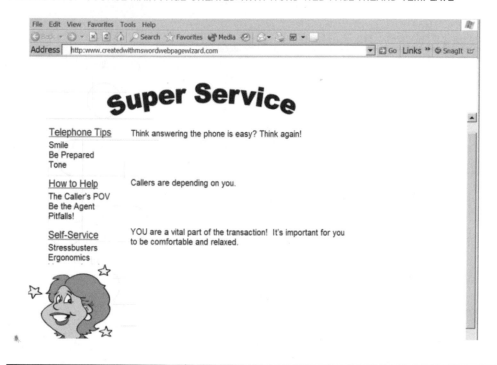

FIGURE 3.11. SAMPLE PAGE OF COURSE CREATED WITH WORD WEB PAGE WIZARD

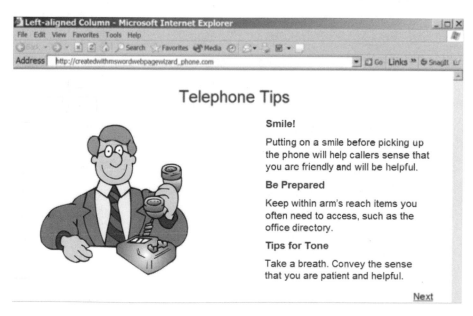

SCORECARD

Web Page Tools Used

Word document: $0
Word art: $0
Clip art from file: $0
Hyperlinks: $0
Total cost: $0

instance, the customer service course shown in the example in Figures 3.10 and 3.11 links to a PowerPoint show that includes audio examples of interactions with difficult customers. It is even possible to insert audio and video objects directly into Word pages ("Insert—Object"), although this will increase the file size significantly.

Word also provides form tools, such as the ones shown in Figure 3.12, that can be added to a Word web page. These forms can be completed and printed out for the learner's use or placement in the employee's file. Note that submitting forms online (rather than just printing them out) requires additional programming on the server hosting the web pages. Consult your IT department or the company hosting your programs for help with this.

The Word Web Page Wizard will automatically create the files and save pages in the format you need for publishing them. Those working from regular Word documents can easily save them as web documents by clicking "File—Save As—Web Page," as shown in Figure 3.13.

Word can be the ideal tool for those needing to create a home page for linking to other programs and can even be used to create a few short e-learning programs (or web-based documents such as the job aids discussed in Chapter Seven). There are limitations, however. Word was designed as a word processing program for creating documents. It wasn't really intended as a web design tool. Programming complex hyperlinking in Word can present quite a challenge; in addition, the web version files are big, especially when they incorporate graphics or media, so they can cause bandwidth and downloading problems.

FIGURE 3.12. EXAMPLES OF FORM TOOLS INSERTED IN A WORD WEB PAGE

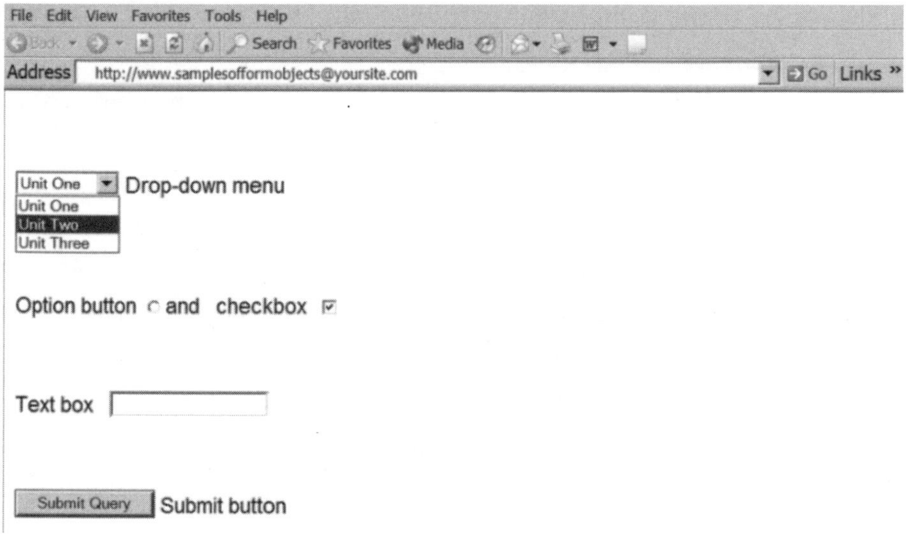

File Edit View Favorites Tools Help

Back · · · Search Favorites Media

Address http://www.samplesofformobjects@yoursite.com ▼ Go Links »

Unit One ▼ Drop-down menu
Unit One
Unit Two
Unit Three

Option button ⊙ and checkbox ☑

Text box [＿＿＿＿＿＿＿]

Submit Query Submit button

FIGURE 3.13. SAVING A WORD DOCUMENT AS A WEB PAGE

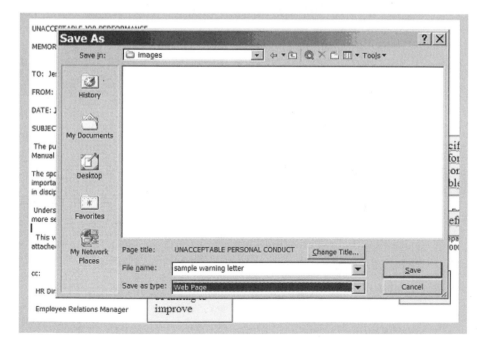

Accessibility

A concern for those creating from-scratch e-learning is accessibility. Section 508 of the Rehabilitation Act presents guidelines for making web documents accessible to all who wish to use them regardless of disability. Those employed by U.S. government organizations that plan to put courses on sites available to the public must ensure that the products are accessible. This can include providing text descriptions of images and audio captioning for video clips.

Converting Microsoft documents to web versions can result in web pages that may not be accessible. Many visually impaired people, for example, use a tool called a screen reader that does exactly that: it "reads" the screen aloud so the person with the visual impairment can hear it. The screen reader reads from the programming code, though, not the page as those with sight would view it. The conversion from Word to web page adds a good deal of extra programming code that can confuse the screen reader, thereby making the page inaccessible to those with a visual impairment. Microsoft does offer help in making documents created with its products more accessible; see http://www.microsoft.com for specifics. Accessibility issues are important for anyone creating e-learning regardless of the products they use for development. For more information, see http://www.section508.gov.

For some training practitioners, Word may be the solution to many problems. Those wishing to build more or longer programs with some animation and more interactivity might find a better shoestring solution with Microsoft PowerPoint or by moving up to the more advanced web design tools discussed in the "Time to Move Up?" section at the end of this chapter.

Microsoft Paint

Many people don't realize they already own a graphics editing program, MS Paint, which comes **free** with the Windows operating system. You can find it by clicking "Start—Programs—Accessories—Paint." Paint can be used to create original images or edit existing images. Paint's tools include items such as a paintbrush, paint bucket, pencil, eraser, and airbrush.

Figure 3.14 shows the original version of an image downloaded from a clip art gallery. Figure 3.15 shows the same image after editing with Paint.

The graphic was reversed using the "Image-Flip" command. Changes to the chalkboard were done by covering the original writing with the paintbrush tool and inserting new text with the text tool. In addition to the changes shown, Paint tools can be used to remove objects from or add elements to a graphic. Similar changes can be made to photographs, including the elimination of "red eye" glare.

FIGURE 3.14. ORIGINAL CLIP ART IMAGE

FIGURE 3.15. IMAGE AFTER EDITING WITH MS PAINT

Paint can also be used for creating screen shots (or "screen captures"). Holding down the computer key Print Window (or Print Screen) in conjunction with the Alt key will take a snapshot of the computer screen and copy it to the clipboard. (On some keyboards, this is done by instead jointly pressing the Print Window and Fn keys.) Open MS Paint and click "Edit—Paste"; the screen shot will appear in the Paint window as shown in Figure 3.16. Free simple software tutorials can be built with PowerPoint using screen shots captured with MS Paint.

FIGURE 3.16. SCREEN SHOT CREATED WITH MS PAINT

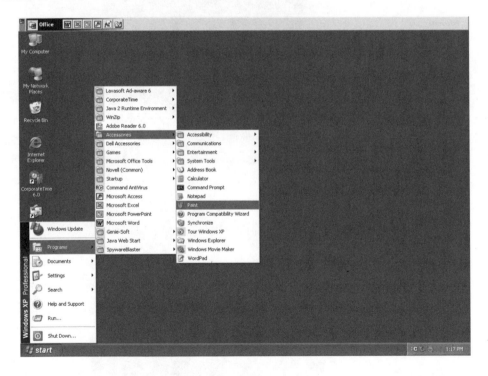

There are many web tutorials on using MS Paint; try searching for "Microsoft paint tutorial" or "learning to use MS Paint." Although Paint does not have all the functionality of a purchased graphics program (which generally cost between $99 and $500), it may be all you need, especially when you're just getting started.

Microsoft Excel and Access

Although Excel and Access are limited in their potential for developing entire e-learning programs, both can be used to support e-learning efforts. Excel, much like PowerPoint, allows extensive hyperlinking, so it can be used both within and in addition to other programs; newer versions of Excel even allow the download and manipulation of web data, such as stock quotes, to the learner's spreadsheet. It can also be used in training requiring computation and in creating tools such as calculators. Access is useful for creating databases to be used by learners. In addition, both products can be used for training functions such as registration and recording completions and test scores. This is discussed further in Chapter Eleven.

Time to Move Up? More Advanced Design Tools

While it's possible to create entire libraries of courses entirely from Power-Point and Word, at some point you may choose to move up to more advanced options. Web page creation tools fall into two general categories. For those willing to learn HTML (HyperText Markup Language, the basic code for developing web materials), there are free and low-cost HTML editors. Other development tools take the form of what are known as WYSIWYG ("what you see is what you get," pronounced "whizzi-wig") tools: the developer types in text and inserts graphics and other elements much as with a basic word processing program. The tool then converts the information into HTML for placement on the web. Many products are available for this; several are discussed below, though you are encouraged to search around and find the tool that you are the most comfortable with.

Microsoft Notepad

Notepad is a simple **free** HTML editor that comes with Windows. (Click on "Start—All Programs—Accessories—Notepad"; if it isn't there, it can be downloaded for

Try searching the web for:

- Web design basics
- Learning web design
- Free web design tutorials
- Beginning web design

free from http://www.notepad.org). Many web designers find this is all they need for creating web pages. Notepad requires knowledge of HTML code, which isn't difficult to learn. (Search the web for "learning HTML" or "HTML tutorial.") Other HTML editors are available for free download from the web, some with more advanced features than Notepad. But since you likely already own Notepad, you may opt to start with it.

How Did They Do It?

Here's a trick for anyone with a little knowledge of HTML. When you're surfing the web and find a page or item you really like, click on the browser toolbar on "View—Source" or "View—Page Source." This will open a box that shows the code for the page you're viewing. It's a great way to learn more about web design and can be a huge cost saver by showing you how to recreate portions of pages you like.

Macromedia Dreamweaver

One of the most popular WYSIWYG programs is Macromedia Dreamweaver (http://www.macromedia.com). Available for commercial use at $399 ($199 for educational or other noncommercial use), Dreamweaver is suited for developing e-learning largely because of Macromedia's extensive **free** support for it. Throughout this book, we'll be looking at free extensions that enable Dreamweaver users to create sophisticated quizzes and tests, set up architecture for an entire website, and even track registrations and learner data such as test scores. Macromedia also offers Dreamweaver for sale as a bundle with its graphics program, Fireworks; its animation program, Flash; and its drawing program, Freehand. The products are available for a free thirty-day trial; excellent tutorials are included even with the trial versions.

Microsoft FrontPage

Microsoft FrontPage is a WYSIWYG tool available for around $200 from Microsoft. Although it is very user friendly, there are a few drawbacks. You probably know that different programs save files with different file extensions.

For instance, Word documents save with the extension .doc (such as "jane.doc"). Web pages similarly have standard file extensions. But web pages created with FrontPage have unusual, nonstandard file extensions that cannot be opened in all browsers. Depending on your situation—for instance, if you are delivering to a small number of learners from within your company's intranet and can work with IT to make sure pages can be viewed—this may not be a concern. Older versions of FrontPage also presented problems in creating web pages accessible to those with disabilities; this is improving with the newer versions, and Microsoft offers assistance on its http://www.microsoft.com site. Finally, pages created in FrontPage tend to have a larger file size than pages built with other products. It is, however, a very easy tool to learn and use, so depending on your situation might be a workable option for your organization.

Site and Authoring Tools

So far we've talked about creating e-learning through developing separate but linked web pages created with an HTML editor. The next level up involves the use of more complete authoring tools that support the development of whole courses and programs. Think of the products we've seen so far as *page* tools. The next level up are better described as *site* tools. While you can certainly create whole courses with your web editing tool (as well as PowerPoint), those planning to develop and launch many different courses will probably want to consider using some kind of site tool.

e-Mail Is Free

When considering deploying inexpensive e-learning, don't forget about e-mail. It can provide support for your courses. After setting up participant mailing lists, you can use your e-mail program to send reminders, distribute pre- or postcourse materials, and offer follow-up comments. Some instructors use the "reply read" tool to monitor whether learners have accessed a particular assignment.

In fact, a new branch of e-learning is emerging specific to the use of e-mail. After all, it's free, it's much less threatening to new e-learners than a more formal-looking online training course, and learners expect less from an e-mail than from a more formal course. A designer can get away with less splash here than in other places. The advent of embedding HTML code into the body of e-mail messages allows sending color, photos, animated graphics, and links to other sites. The newest advance in e-mail is voice e-mail, in which the sender can embed a brief spoken message.

If you need to get an urgent piece of information—for example, a change in a step of a procedure—to a thousand employees at once, you might be able to use a good e-mail message in place of training at all. When seeking to maximize use of the "already-haves" in your e-learning tool kit, remember that e-mail is free, easily accessible, and comfortable for many learners.

Macromedia Learning Site. Among the **free** extensions available to Dreamweaver users is Macromedia's Learning Site tool. Learning Site provides basic architectural structure, like preset choices for navigation, and allows you to build three different types of interactive pages. Basically it lets the designer set up plans for a course and fill in content later. We will be looking at Macromedia's Learning Site and its companion, the **free** Coursebuilder tool, throughout this book; together they provide quizzing and testing options and can even support the student data tracking process.

Authoring Products. A number of sophisticated authoring tools allow the designer to create complex, higher-end e-learning programs. Well-known products include Authorware, ReadyGo! Dazzlermax, and Toolbook. All of these have good track records and good support, though some may fall beyond the reach of those working on a shoestring budget. The learning curve for authoring products can be long, and organizations just starting out may not have the in-house technical expertise needed to support them.

A Free Alternative: Online Communities. Several commercial sites offer **free** virtual communities. Popular sources are Yahoo Groups (http://www.yahoo.com) and MSN Groups (http://www.msn.com). Setting up a course site takes a matter of minutes and requires no knowledge of HTML code or web design. The basic structure is a customizable main page with links to supporting pages where the developer can store files, such as Word documents or PowerPoint shows (these can be created as regular documents and do not have to be built as web pages) that contain learning content and training material. Most online communities also offer message boards, chat, and calendars that can be set to auto-send reminders and information about assignments, and a polling feature for creating student tests and quizzes. The designer can choose to make the site password protected. Although online communities are more commonly used to structure a single course, some organizations use virtual communities to support whole organizational training programs. Because the site is hosted by the provider, the organization has no development or hosting costs, so use really is completely free. The only drawback is that communities are ad-supported, which means learners logging in may be greeted by an ad on the welcome page or the message board. The main page of a virtual community site looks something like the one shown in Figure 3.17.

FIGURE 3.17. SAMPLE HOME PAGE FROM FREE VIRTUAL COMMUNITY SITE

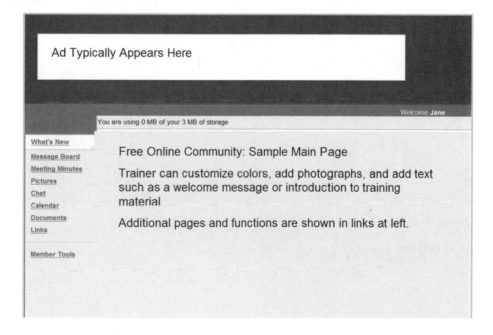

For an even more basic solution, some providers offer simple ad-supported free sites. Yahoo's Geocities service, for example, allows users to create their own websites with a home page and a few supplemental pages. These sites do not, however, provide functions available through the community option, such as password protection and discussion boards.

An Inexpensive Alternative: Quia Class Pages. Other products we'll be looking at throughout this book come from http://www.quia.com. Better known for its templates for creating quizzes and game-show-type games, Quia offers users the option of creating class pages on which to list items such as assignments, instructor comments, and links to other sites. Quia hosts the page on its server and sends the designer a URL (the Uniform Resource Locator, or web address) for his or her page. An annual subscription includes access to all the Quia services. It costs $49 a year for educational use and $99 a year for other use.

Summary

Creating inexpensive e-learning is often not so much a matter of technical wizardry as the ability and willingness to be resourceful and creative; the tools necessary for development of basic programs are within easy reach. In the next chapter, we'll look at enhancing basic programs with free and inexpensive add-ons.

Enhancing Basic Programs

THE TOOLS WE DISCUSSED in Chapter Three can give you a good start in developing inexpensive e-learning solutions. E-learning designers need to be careful, though, about ending up with a text-only wall of words. Take advantage of the many free and low-cost tools that add visual interest, interactivity, and media to programs. This chapter looks at inexpensive ways of enhancing e-learning courses with art and other media, as well as design strategies that support learning and provide interaction with training content.

Free Clip Art and Other Media

Try as much as possible to use what you have. The Microsoft Office products have a one-click link to extensive clip art and photo galleries and sound effects and music libraries. Elsewhere on the web are whole libraries of **free** graphics, including animated images, and free audio clips like movie quotes. These can be found on such sites as http://www.animfactory.com

and http://www.thefreesite.com, and the home pages of several search engines, including http://www.altavista.com and http://www.google, offer links for searching for free audio, video, and images, including add-ons like banners and buttons.

Some words of caution: most sites offering free or low-cost products (including the Microsoft clip art gallery site) provide them with the understanding that they are only for personal use or for use on websites. Some have restrictions regarding commercial use and use in other materials, like logos or printed matter; some request that a credit line be included with the image or other object. Before using

Try searching the web for:

- Free clip art
- Free sound effects
- Free web buttons

any product, check the site's requirements, which usually appear at the bottom of the home page as a link called "terms of use" or "legal."

Also, it is an unfortunate reality that not all sites are safe. Be careful about downloading items from an unknown source. Identify reputable or well-known sources of materials; use antivirus scans before installing, running, or opening files on your computer; and ask for guidance from IT experts. Depending on your needs, you may find that a subscription to an inexpensive all-purpose art, media, and code service is worth the peace of mind of knowing that the products you want to use are safe.

Free Design Templates

Design templates can make it much easier to create web pages and programs. In addition to being great time-savers they can be huge cost savers. They give a site a consistent look and feel and can support ease of navigation. The web is full of sites offering free design templates for web pages. There are hundreds of free PowerPoint background templates on the web too, though several dozen come with PowerPoint itself. By way of example, Figure 4.1 shows some of the free templates offered by http://www.elated.com. downloadable as page kits, which include templates for a site's main page and complemen-

FIGURE 4.1. SOME FREE WEB PAGE TEMPLATES AVAILABLE FROM ELATED.COM

Source: Used with permission of Elated.

Aperture.
A cute center-framed template inspired by cameras and photography. Slick modern fonts!

View PageKit
Download PageKit

GE-OM.
Wacky grid patterns and extreeeme perspectives! Lovely two-tone orange theme, too.

View PageKit
Download PageKit

Perfect.
Funky typography, complete menu control, and all-round groovesomeness.

View PageKit
Download PageKit

Hi.
Clean as a whistle, loads of customization possible, and of course, lovely to boot!
View PageKit
Download PageKit

Washed.
It's another info-heavy 'Kit, nonframed, with a real 21st century design to it.

View PageKit
Download PageKit

Tune!
Our first music-based 'Kit, fraemeset-based, and with a load of fantastic ideas and lots of color.

View PageKit
Download PageKit

Demographic.
A nice bold template that really brings home the message. Cool chunky fonts.

Uncle.
A slick, lively yet understated template, very arty. Great for small screen resolutions too.

Hardaportal.
Information heavy page layout and total menu control with stylesheets!

tary subpages. Elated also offers business-oriented templates for complete websites at reasonable prices (see www.pagekits.com). And for a small fee, it will help you modify the templates should you want to make changes.

When presented with so many sites offering free or inexpensive products, you may find it useful to find and stick with a few favorites. Every site's products seem to have their own quirks. I like templates from www.elated. com partly because they're easy to use but also because I like the Elated attitude. Elated's mission statement reads: "Elated is dedicated to delivering top-quality, original web-building resources in a down-to-earth, friendly and helpful way. Our mission is to serve our community of beginner, intermediate and advanced Webmasters, and to work to strengthen that community."

Free Interactivity Tools

Dozens of sites offer free interactivity products available for download, from games, file management programs, and flowcharting software to media players, phone servers, and software for animating GIF images. Free survey and polling tools are also widely available. (Sites offering these products often describe it as either freeware or shareware, and there is a difference. *Freeware* is usually an early, prototypical version of yet-to-be-released software or is material created by a developer willing to give it away. *Shareware* may be a completely free download, but often is something offered for a trial period, is given free only with limited capability as compared to the full version, or eventually requires registration or purchase. The advantage is that it does allow the user to try it before buying.)

> Try searching the web for these items, typing the following phrases into your browser's search window (use the plus sign where indicated):
>
> • Free web templates
> • Web design tools + free
> • Free web design tools and templates

Elsewhere on the web you'll find sites offering free snippets of JavaScript code. These add functionality to web pages; you can insert such tools as site hit counters, calculators, status bars showing progress while a media clip loads, communication tools such as message boards, and even password protection for courses and search tools for your site. (Advanced web page tools such as Dreamweaver allow easy creation of some JavaScript interactions as well.)

From the free sites, you simply copy and paste the code into your web page. (Take care to be sure that the information you're using is safe.) This takes just a little knowledge of HTML code; there are many free web tutorials on using JavaScript as well. In Chapter Five we'll also look at free or low-cost products that will auto-program more elaborate JavaScript actions so you can easily create your own quizzes and games.

Free Microsoft Downloads

Microsoft offers dozens of **free** downloads in support of its products, from the Windows media player to tools for digital photography. Three programs—Microsoft Agent, Windows MovieMaker, and Microsoft Producer—are especially useful for those seeking to enhance e-learning courses.

Microsoft Agent

Apart from providing interest and entertainment, the thoughtful use of characters, also known as *agents,* can improve the learning experience. Clark and Mayer (2003) describe two studies in which learners interacting with an online agent performed significantly better on transfer tests than did learners in no-agent groups. The best-known program for online characters is Microsoft Agent. Available at http://www.Microsoft.com/products/msagent, Microsoft provides several animated, talking characters that can be used to create training agents for use in web pages. Figure 4.2 shows an agent used in a tutorial for the new employee timekeeping system.

It is possible to incorporate Microsoft Agent characters into PowerPoint presentations as well. A product called Vox Proxy®, available at http://www.voxproxy.com, greatly simplifies this process and gives choices of characters in addition to those provided by Microsoft.

Search around on the web for ideas about using agents. You'll find characters such as a detective who helps unravel the "mystery" of the shipping process, a travel agent working with an online fare calculator, and "Sweet Auntie Marie" walking the learner through online cooking classes.

FIGURE 4.2. ONLINE AGENT INCORPORATED INTO TUTORIAL ON EMPLOYEE TIMEKEEPING

Source: Scientist character used with permission of Right Seat Software, Inc., Golden, Colorado, USA.

To facilitate the ease of incorporating the characters into online programs, Microsoft Agent uses text-to-speech technology. This allows the designer to simply type in narration that the character then says aloud. Simple gestures like smiling or waving can be programmed by copying and pasting HTML code available on the Microsoft Agent site. In order to hear the characters talk, users must have text-to-speech engines enabled on their machines. This isn't really a big issue but might require help from IT specialists and could prove problematic for those designing for far-flung users. Despite this and a couple of other small drawbacks (for instance, computerized voices still sound computerized), Microsoft Agent is a great **free** tool.

There are extensive resources available for those wishing to use Microsoft Agent, from tutorials and other support to dozens of additional characters. In addition to the Agent site, try a web search to locate the many other characters, ideas, and support out there.

Too, recurring characters serve as familiar icons to the learner. These do not necessarily have to be animated talking agents such as the ones available through Microsoft. You could certainly create your own with still photos or other images.

Agents are meant to enhance your e-learning program. As with most other tools, the overuse of agents can irritate learners and undermine the intent of the training program. Use them judiciously; take care that comments, tone, and quality of voice are not annoying; and if possible, give learners the option of turning the agents off.

Windows MovieMaker

If you have access to a digital video camera or already own video training materials, the Windows MovieMaker program will allow you to create professional-looking custom video complete with animated titles and credit slides. The program, available for **free** at http://www.microsoft.com/windowsxp/using/moviemaker/default.mspx (it automatically downloads with the Windows Service Pack 2 installation), breaks a digital video clip into smaller clips that can be clicked and dragged to a storyboard. You can rearrange the sequence, edit individual clips, and add narration, music, and animated titles. And MovieMaker is very user friendly. It is a relatively new product, so you will need access to a computer with Windows ME or XP to use it. Figure 4.3 shows an example of a video clip broken into frames by MovieMaker. And Figure 4.4 shows a storyboard with selected clips and titles added. This can be saved as a new video file.

If you are working with a videotape, you'll have to first convert it from tape (analog) to a digital format. This used to be an expensive undertaking but can now be done directly from a VCR to a computer with a video capture card or by using an external video capture device, which can now be had

---

FIGURE 4.3. USING MOVIEMAKER TO BREAK VIDEO INTO CLIPS

Example 1 008

Example 1 009

Example 1 010

Example 1 011

Example 1 015

Example 1 016

Example 1 017

Example 1 018

FIGURE 4.4. MOVIEMAKER STORYBOARD SHOWING REARRANGED CLIPS AND ADDED TITLES

for less than $100. Newer videotape cameras can also handle the conversion process, as can the combination DVD-R/VCR machines now available for less than $250.

Microsoft Producer

This **free** add-on to PowerPoint allows the user to capture and synchronize PowerPoint slides with audio, video, "talking head" presentations, and other images. Some organizations use this exclusively as their "authoring" tool. The product can be downloaded at http://www.microsoft.com/windows/windowsmedia/technologies/producer.aspx. The site offers a library of case studies complete with examples of finished programs.

Enhancing Programs with Audio and Video

To access audio and video files, learner machines need sound cards, speakers, and a media player. Also called *plug-ins,* players are available for free download and often come already installed on computers. Popular plug-ins are Microsoft's Windows Media Player and Apple's QuickTime player. Although both handle most types of media files, each is more fully functional with the system for which it was originally developed. Because different audio and video software creation and editing programs generate different kinds of media files, it's important to know what type of player your learners will be using. An alternative for those wishing to incorporate video into e-learning programs is to export clips in the Flash format (you may need to get some help from a Flash expert for this). These clips will play back on any machine with the free Flash player installed.

In using audio and video, realize that inexpensive speakers often come without volume controls; your e-learning program should have a built-in volume control so learners can adjust the sound. File size is also a concern when using multimedia. Although audio files are large, software for compressing and editing sound can be had for as little as $60. Video editing software will also compress files. An additional means of reducing file size is to break video into short segments of instruction and use each piece as a stand-alone clip.

Although repurposing existing video can be an excellent means of saving money on e-learning development, creating custom video is another matter altogether. There is generally no more expensive development undertaking than writing and shooting video from scratch. While good in-house actors can help save on costs, shooting professional-looking homemade video is remarkably time-consuming, and professional video services are costly. Review the objectives of your e-learning program. Do you have to have video? Is there an alternative? For instance, can you substitute still photos with voice added over? Consider whether the benefit of having the video is worth the resources it will consume.

Macromedia Coursebuilder

Among the support tools provided by Macromedia is the wonderful Coursebuilder product. You can download it from http://www.macromedia.com as a **free** extension for Dreamweaver, and it works well. Although it's meant primarily as a quiz-making tool (which we'll discuss in depth in Chapter Five), one of the items included with the Coursebuilder download is scripting for a slider interaction (shown in figures 4.5 and 4.6.) that can add interactivity while maximizing available space on a web page. Additional text or images are revealed as the slide tool is moved across the page. The slider also provides a break from the typical click-to-the-next-screen action so often seen in e-learning programs. Information is stored as separate layers of text that are revealed when the slider is released at particular spots. Figures 4.5 and 4.6 show a Coursebuilder slider used to present information on managing employee performance problems. The text changes as the slider is moved along the bar.

FIGURE 4.5. EXAMPLE OF A COURSEBUILDER SLIDER

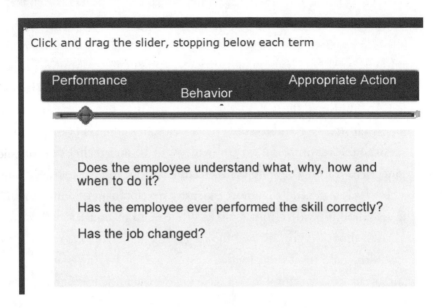

FIGURE 4.6. SLIDER INTERACTION

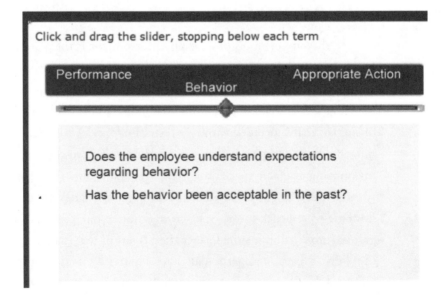

HTML/DHTML/XML?

Learning about e-learning brings with it a flurry of acronyms and computerese. HTML is the basic code for creating web pages. The next level up is Dynamic HTML (DHTML), which is a combination of HTML, JavaScript, and other elements called cascading style sheets and the document object model. Putting these together allows more interactivity on a web page. XML is code that tells the computer what kind of document has been created—that is, whether the web page is a table of contents for a book, a cake recipe, or a collection of case studies for a training course. It probably isn't necessary for you to know much more about DHTML or XML right now, but because you'll likely run into the terms it's good to have some familiarity with them.

Design Tips and Tricks

When creating programs, sometimes just using interesting **free** design strategies can help enhance the program by encouraging interest and engagement. These include the thoughtful use of themes and metaphors, lists of sites for further study, and programming tricks that help break the monotony so common to "click-along" programs.

Themes and Metaphors

A theme or metaphor can serve as a unifying element, add interest, and even reduce the need for some content. Figure 4.7 shows an example from a supervisory skills program that uses a "boot camp" metaphor, including graphics of cartoon soldiers and a foot-locker-lettering–style font for headings. The images tie the program together as well as support the concept that the course is meant as basic training for new supervisors their first few days on the job. It's not intended to be exhaustive, just an overview.

FIGURE 4.7. USE OF METAPHOR IN AN ONLINE TRAINING PROGRAM

BASIC TRAINING FOR NEW SUPERVISORS

Click on an image to choose a module:

 MOTIVATING EMPLOYEES

 DISCIPLINARY ACTION PROCESS

 PERFORMANCE MANAGEMENT

Other common themes include the idea of an adventure or a journey, such as "the maze of court proceedings" and "budget process safari"; solving a "puzzle" or "mystery"; and working from a "recipe."

Site Samplers and Hot Lists

A site sampler (also known as a subject sampler) does just what it says: allows learners to "taste" a number of ideas and sites. A sampler is good for the learner who finished a course but wants more information, who isn't sure whether the subject matter will be of interest to her, or who likes to "surf," or leap from idea to idea. It can also facilitate self-directed learning by encouraging trainees to pursue lines of thinking that are of special interest to them. The sampler shown in Figure 4.8, the concluding page in a course on the organization's hiring process, links to in-house resources such as Word documents from classroom training programs and information from the organization's human resource department.

FIGURE 4.8. EXAMPLE OF A SITE SAMPLER

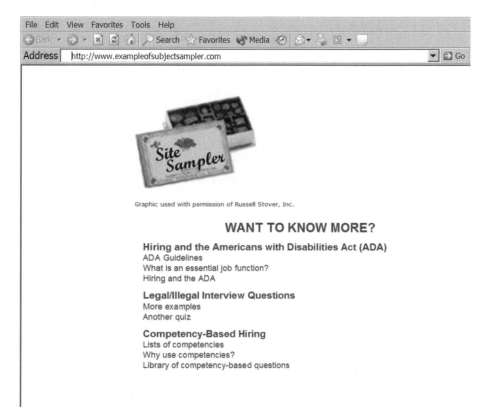

The hot list is a more focused, structured version of the subject sampler. This is a list of sites that support an assignment or directed learning activity. For instance, you might give diversity workshop participants a list of good links that focus on the experience of first-generation American Latinos.

Those working with tight budgets will find site samplers and hot lists good free tools for extending basic e-learning programs and a way of including the "nice-to-know" training content in addition to the "must know." The only drawback to using samplers and hot lists is the need to frequently check links, especially those to external sites, to ensure they are still working and the information there is current.

Hot Spots

Hot spots (or hot objects) are easy ways of adding interactivity to programs. The hot areas call up an object such as an image or pop-up box of text, or take the learner to another web page or topic area. As with the Coursebuilder slider interaction, hot spots can help maximize the use of screen "real estate" since a good deal of information can be placed on one web page without the appearance of clutter. The actions give learners some control over which items they view and in what order. Hot spots are often used in e-learning to create materials such as, for instance, a clickable "map" showing the location of items in a store or names of parts of an engine.

For use in web pages, the hot spot is created with JavaScript. Creating it is a simple one-click task when using web page tools like Dreamweaver. Those using other page creation or authoring products can download the tools for generating the necessary JavaScript free from the web. Similar hot-spot effects can be created in PowerPoint by setting hyperlinks from the first image to another slide containing the new image.

Figures 4.9 and 4.10 show examples of hot spots.

Summary

Moving from text-heavy programs to those that are more visually and kinesthetically interesting needn't be an expensive proposition. Creative, resourceful designers can find many low-cost ways of adding to basic pages. In Chapter Five, we'll look at programs that incorporate more advanced interactive strategies: quizzes, games, searches, puzzles, and simulations.

FIGURE 4.9. TEXT IS REVEALED AS MOUSE IS ROLLED OVER HOT SPOTS

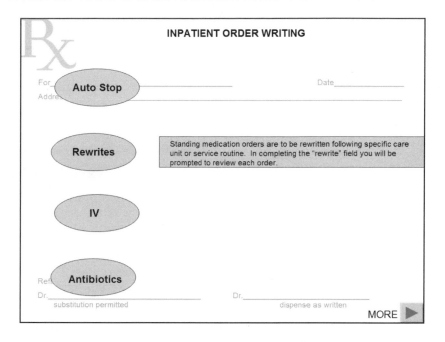

FIGURE 4.10. CLICKABLE MAP WITH HOT SPOT

Creating Inexpensive Quizzes, Games, Searches, Puzzles, and Simulations

THE USE OF QUIZZING AND OTHER interactive strategies can turn the deadly dull into the engaging and the too-much-text to entertaining. It breaks the tedium of dry content, gives opportunities to practice using new information, and can be designed to give built-in rewards for learners. Most important, providing opportunities for learners to interact with material in a meaningful way facilitates application of information and transfer back on the job. This chapter offers an overview of free and low-cost ways of creating quizzes, games, searches, puzzles, and simulations.

Quizzes

Quizzes give learners the opportunity to assess their understanding and gauge their progress, encourage them to review course materials if necessary, and help them determine their readiness to move on to new material. This chapter discusses quizzes and games primarily as self-study aids and tools to enhance interactivity and engagement. With the exception of PowerPoint, all of the quiz and game tools referred to offer basic tracking of scores at varying prices. (Tracking and reporting of data such as test scores is covered in depth in Chapter Eleven.) We'll look first at several quiz-making tools and then at some examples of the products they can be used to create.

Tools for Creating Quizzes

The training professional working on a shoestring has the option of using a number of free and low-cost quiz tools, including PowerPoint, Macromedia's Coursebuilder, Hot Potatoes, and Quia. Other similar tools can be found by searching the web for "free quiz making software," though many of these offer less support in terms of tutorials and other resources.

PowerPoint. Simple true-false and multiple-choice quiz questions can be created with PowerPoint. Through the use of hyperlinking, the quiz allows learners to choose a response, after which they are taken to another slide for feedback, additional information, or the next question.

Macromedia Coursebuilder. Among the support tools provided by Macromedia is the Coursebuilder product. Available from http://www.macromedia.com as a **free** extension for the Dreamweaver web page tool, Coursebuilder allows the designer to create several types of quiz questions, including multiple choice and true-false, as well as more complex interactions such as the drag-and-drop. Use of these more sophisticated interactions provides more interest and learner control than the usual click-on-the-button action. In addition, Coursebuilder provides a timer tool that can be programmed to let learners know how much time they have left or how much time has elapsed, or to disable the quiz after a given time period has elapsed.

Coursebuilder is an excellent tool but can be rather challenging to learn. An excellent resource is Garin Hess and Steven Hancock's *Using Dreamweaver to Create e-Learning* (2001). Much of the book focuses on step-by-step instructions for creating Coursebuilder interactions and includes a CD with narrated tutorials and animated examples to walk users through the process.

Hot Potatoes. Hot Potatoes, developed by the University of Victoria and sold through the Half-Baked Software company (http://web.uvic.ca/hrd/halfbaked), provides a half-dozen exercises including several quiz formats as well as crossword puzzles. The software is available **free** to nonprofit organizations and sold to other businesses for only $100. Hot Potatoes is easy to use: the designer enters text and otherwise works by pasting and clicking, though some knowledge of web design can be helpful for enhancing the finished look. The Hot Potatoes site offers extensive resources, including good tutorials and a library of finished sample quizzes.

Quia.   Quia (http://www.quia.com), better known for its game creation tools (discussed later in this chapter), offers a variety of formats for online quizzes, such as matching, true-false, and multiple choice. The Quia annual subscription ($49 for educational institutions and $99 for businesses) provides access to all the Quia products, including the quiz and game templates, tracking of scores, and customizable class pages.

Quia differs from other items discussed here in that it is a service rather than a product. Whereas Coursebuilder and Hot Potatoes are software to install, Quia is entirely externally hosted. You would, for instance, create your matching quiz in Hot Potatoes with your own web page tool and upload it to your own server space. A similar Quia quiz will remain on the Quia site with a unique web address Quia assigns to you. This can be an advantage for those who need hosting services or are using Quia's class page as a home base for the training program. Others may find it a drawback in that learners must be sent to the quiz at the external link provided by Quia, then come back to the online program. This may not be of any concern to you but is an issue to be aware of as it could factor into your decision of which quiz-making tools to use.

Types of Quizzes

These tools can be used to create a number of familiar quiz types. With any of them, you can develop items in true-false and multiple-choice formats. Matching and fill-in-the-blank quizzes can be developed with Excel, Coursebuilder, Quia, and Hot Potatoes, and Coursebuilder also provides the option of creating essay response quizzes, drag-and-drop activities, and quizzes using slider interaction (see Chapter Four). The more sophisticated interactions use JavaScript and DHTML automatically generated by the quiz program.

True-False. The true-false format is one of the easiest to create. Figure 5.1 illustrates how to construct a true-false quiz using PowerPoint.

FIGURE 5.1. TRUE-FALSE QUIZ CREATED WITH POWERPOINT

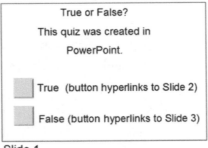

Multiple Choice. Simple multiple-choice quizzes can be developed with PowerPoint by adding more choices on the main slide supplemented by additional corresponding answer slides. For a more sophisticated quiz, both Hot Potatoes and Coursebuilder provide multiple-choice formats with complex progressive or scaffolded feedback (more meaningful than just text that says "correct"), which can give learners the chance to figure things out for themselves. This can take the form of hints and feedback that lead to remediation or additional information. Figures 5.2 through 5.4 show a multiple-choice interaction in which several of the choices are incorrect. The learner receives progressive feedback based on his or her responses.

FIGURE 5.2. FEEDBACK PROVIDED FOR FIRST INCORRECT ANSWER

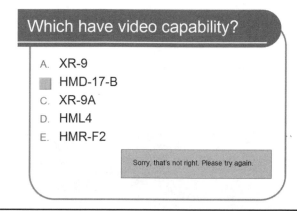

FIGURE 5.3. ADDITIONAL FEEDBACK SHOWN FOR SECOND INCORRECT ANSWER

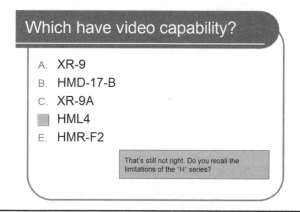

FIGURE 5.4. FEEDBACK FOR THIRD INCORRECT ANSWER DIRECTS LEARNER TO REMEDIATION MATERIAL

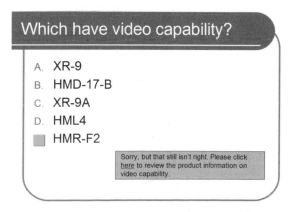

Another type of multiple-choice quiz can be created using the Coursebuilder slider interaction. Figures 5.5 and 5.6 show a quiz in which the learner slides the bar to choose among options given as a numerical range.

FIGURE 5.5. INITIAL PRESENTATION OF QUESTION USING COURSEBUILDER'S SLIDER INTERACTION

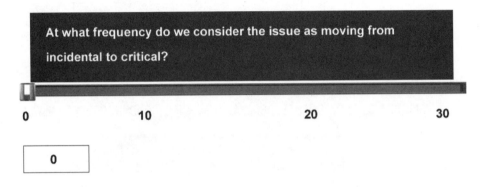

FIGURE 5.6. RESULT WHEN LEARNER SLIDES BAR TO CORRECT RESPONSE

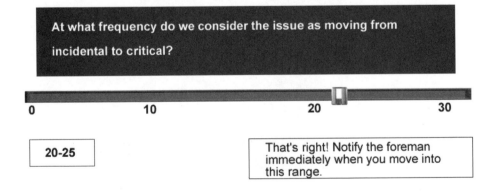

Fill in the Blank. Creative use of the fill-in-the blank approach can be surprisingly interesting and challenging. Figures 5.7 and 5.8 show examples of fill-in-the-blank quizzes built with Hot Potatoes. Figure 5.8 also includes a video clip that allows students of a foreign language to see lip movements as well as hear the words spoken.

FIGURE 5.7. MATHEMATICAL QUIZ PRESENTED IN FILL-IN-THE-BLANK FORMAT

Exercise: Calculation of interest and reserves

Account: Jeff Smith, Lazy Acres

Terms: Payment within 30 days— 2% discount
Date of payment: 30 days

Date	Voucher	Target $	Credit $	Days	Interest
1/20/04	JB 867	11,500			
2/14/04	JB 1198	23,750			
4/02/04	JB 1487	18,500			

All demands are to be settled by 6/16/04 with 7.5% interest to be paid.

What is the sum of the interest numbers? ☐

What is the interest divisor? ☐

How high is the amount of total claim to 6/16/04? ☐

Debit	Amount $	Credit	Amount $

FIGURE 5.8. FILL-IN-THE-BLANK FOREIGN LANGUAGE VOCABULARY QUIZ

Source: Used with permission of the Ashcombe School, Surrey, England.

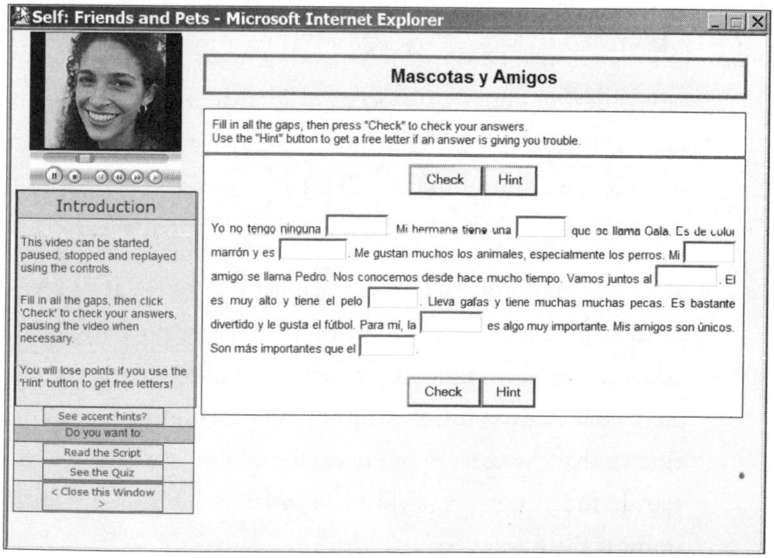

An issue in using fill-in-the-blank interactions is the need to anticipate every possible correct answer. In creating the interaction, the designer must "tell" the program how to score the quiz so the learner can receive feedback. For instance, suppose an online quiz on employment hiring has a fill-in-the blank question for which the correct answer is *interview*. It's an awkward word to type and is easy to misspell. If the objective is to test whether the learner knows that "interview" is the appropriate way to clarify information about the applicant's work history (rather than to test the learner's typing or spelling ability), the program will need to be set up to score as correct anything close to "interview"—for example, *interveiw, interviews, interveiews, interviewing,* and *interveiwing*. The developer will also need to anticipate issues with synonyms: for instance, *capital* and *investment funds* may mean the same thing to learners. (Notice that in Figure 5.7, the designer used the fill-in-the-blank format for mathematical questions—for which there was only one correct answer.)

Essay. It is possible to create questions requiring an essay-type response. As with the fill-in-the-blank format, complications arise from the need to evaluate the answers. This can be done in one of two ways: by "telling" the program to grade the answers or by having the answers submit to a person who will read and grade them. Either way, the designer must establish extended, clear criteria for how responses will be evaluated. An alternative to having responses scored is to have the learner type an answer and then compare it to an example of a correct response that appears on the next screen or a smaller pop-up screen.

Matching. The matching quiz is useful for testing items such as knowledge of terminology, ordering steps in a process, or identifying parts of a machine. It can be created in Coursebuilder using drop-down menus with a choice of answers, or in either Coursebuilder or Hot Potatoes as a matching-terms activity, as shown in Figure 5.9.

Drag and Drop. Drag-and-drop exercises are a great way to teach a process, steps in a procedure, or tasks that involve ordering. Figure 5.10 shows a drag-and-drop activity used for training new bagging clerks at a grocery store. This was created with Coursebuilder, which allows the designer to program the interaction so that the user cannot make a mistake. It won't "let" the learner put the eggs in first, for example, but will instead snap the eggs back to their starting point if the learner tries to perform incorrectly.

FIGURE 5.9. MATCHING QUIZ CREATED WITH HOT POTATOES

Match the terms by typing the letter inside the box with the corresponding answer. When you are finished click on "check" to check your answers.

☐	Washout	A. Total lack of oxygen
☐	Radical	B. Cleansing or sweeping clean
☐	Anoxia	C. Childbirth
☐	Parturition	D. Directed to the cause
☐	Ganglion	E. Group of nerve cell bodies located outside the central nervous system

CHECK

FIGURE 5.10. DRAG-AND-DROP QUIZ CREATED WITH COURSEBUILDER

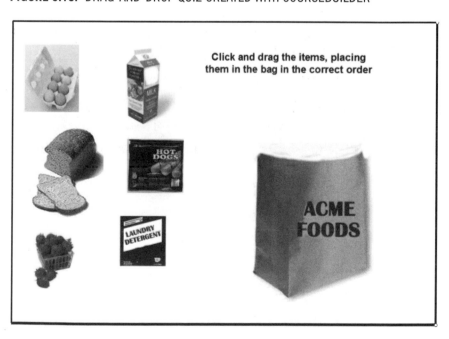

Click and drag the items, placing them in the bag in the correct order

Games

Why use a game? There are lots of reasons: games can encourage transfer of learning, provide stimulation and variety, break up monotony, provide the means for delivering information that otherwise might appear as plain text on a screen, and serve to offer what training expert William Horton (http://www.horton.com) calls "a seductive test." Some simple online training games are variations on the quiz formats just discussed. Others borrow from familiar childhood games like paper-and-pencil activities such as tic-tac-toe and hangman, from card games like Concentration and Solitaire, and from TV game shows like *Jeopardy* and *Who Wants to Be a Millionaire?*

Tools for Creating Games

Although they require a good deal of up-front thought and planning, good games can be created at minimal cost and go a long way toward enhancing e-learning programs. They can be built with a number of tools from already-haves like e-mail and PowerPoint to free or inexpensive Flash game templates.

e-Mail. Training expert Sivasailam Thiagarajan (better known as "Thiagi") considers it his life's work to create a game a day. The information below is taken from Thiagi's website (http://www.thiagi.com) and is used with his permission. The website is a rich source of practical ideas and suggestions, with weekly updates and a free monthly newsletter. Among Thiagi's many contributions to the field are a number of **free**, easy e-mail games. Here are a few:

• "101 Tips": Participants are given a deadline for submitting tips (not to exceed seventy-five words) on topics like "ensuring a safe environment for learners," "characteristics of an effective presenter," "motivating employees," "selling to the reluctant customer," or "making patients feel at ease." At the end of the game, a panel of judges selects the top three tips and sends those back out to the participants. A variation of the game is to award points for tips with the top three winners declared at the end.

• "Four Heads": In round 1, the trainer sends four minicases to four participants and asks each to come up with a solution. In round 2, the trainer sends one solution to two participants. One is asked to write a critique, noting the weaknesses of the solution, and the other is to write a testimonial attesting to its strengths. This is repeated with the remaining three original solutions (so the total now is four original solutions sent to eight recipients). In round 3, the original solution, its critique, and its testimonial go to still another participant, who refines the solution to a final state. This is repeated with the other three solutions. The final products are sent to all participants.

• "Relay": The instructor sends a message to one participant that says, "The characteristics of a good supervisor are [fill in the blank]." The recipient adds a short comment and then forwards the message to the next participant. (Those versed in adult education theory might recognize this as a variation of the "ink shedding" technique.) The last participant forwards the whole thread to the instructor, who can choose to consolidate the messages, further process the responses, award points, or do something else. Other similar relay games can be played by prompting learners with initial messages based on the course material such as "Best of _____ ," "Best Practices in _____ ," "Characteristics of _____ ," and "Ideas for _____ ."

Table 5.1 summarizes the advantages and disadvantages of e-mail games.

TABLE 5.1. ADVANTAGES AND DISADVANTAGES OF E-MAIL GAMES

Advantages	Disadvantages
Free	Play can be slow
No new skills required for learner	No visually engaging elements like animation
E-mail can be accessed from many locations on any computer with Internet access	Cannot be played alone
No need for programming or authoring	Easy for messages and instructions to get lost among the spam
Game easy to access: no log-in, password, plug-in, download	Players have varying levels of interest and involvement; plan for dropouts
Can involve learners from all over the world within the span of one day	

Flash and Java Game Templates. Several vendors offer Flash and Java game templates
for free or at very reasonable prices. The formats can be used to provide a
fairly sophisticated finished product that can include hard-to-program features like scoring and timekeeping. Figure 5.11 shows an example of a Flash
game created from a template offered by Collaborative Learning Systems
(http://www.collaborativelearningsystems.com) in which the learner is asked
to choose whether the question is legal or illegal. Note that the game is based
on the true-false quiz format; the addition of scoring and a running clock
encourages engagement and provides more visual interest than would a more
traditionally formatted true-false test.

FIGURE 5.11. GAME CREATED WITH COLLABORATIVE LEARNING SYSTEMS GAME TEMPLATE

Used with permission of Collaborative Learning Systems.

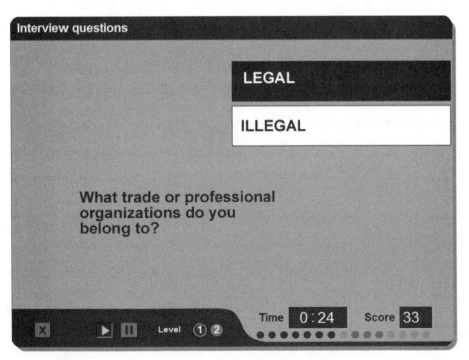

For the Flash games, users need the Flash player, which is already installed on most newer machines and available for free from http://www.macromedia. com. Java (not to be confused with JavaScript) games run in programs called *applets,* which require a plug-in. This is also often already available on machines; if it is not, the download is available for free from http://www. java.com.

Collaborative Learning Systems provides a choice of Flash game templates. The one shown in Figure 5.11 allows you to choose colors to match your own site's color scheme, write the questions, determine how many levels of difficulty to offer, and set the amount of time allowed for responding. The e-games' minimum price is $18.00 for ten published games, a cost of only $1.80 per game, regardless of the number of users. You can create as many games as you like, which the company will host on its server while you are working on them. Your account is charged only for the games you publish by saving them to your hard drive; you can then insert them into any—and as many—web pages you like. Collaborative Learning Systems provides extensive step-by-step tutorials to make learning the process relatively easy.

Another popular source of both Flash and Java games is Quia (http:// www.quia.com). Quia offers templates for sixteen activities, including online games similar to some popular television game shows. The use of such games has a couple of advantages: the familiar format makes them easy for users to learn and play, as well as making fans of the shows more likely to give them a try. The Quia subscription is $99 per year ($49 for education entities) for unlimited use of all the templates; the company currently offers a free thirty-day trial. The Quia website contains tutorials and its showcase of many games on assorted topics and is a good source of inspiration for designers. Figures 5.12 through 5.14 show an example of a game created using Quia.

FIGURE 5.12. FIRST SCREEN OF QUIA GAME SHOW–TYPE GAME

Source: Used with permission of Quia (www.quia.com).

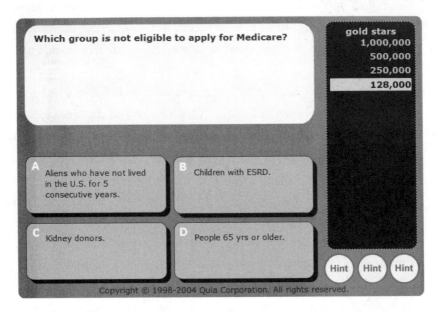

FIGURE 5.13. QUIA SCREEN SHOWING HINT

Source: Used with permission of Quia (www.quia.com).

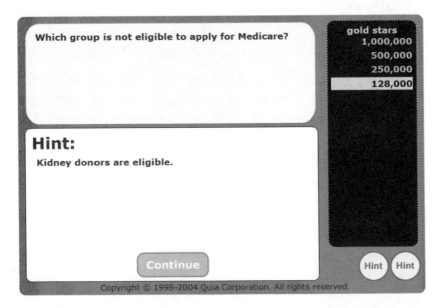

FIGURE 5.14. QUIA SCREEN SHOWING PROGRESSION TO NEXT QUESTION

Source: Used with permission of Quia (www.quia.com).

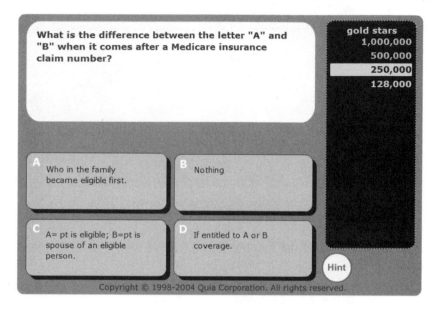

SCORECARD

"*Millionaire*"-type game built with software from a commercial web game vendor:

Comes with several customizable templates so you can add in your own content.

Installed on 1 computer: $795

Installed on 10 computers: $3,995

Installed on 100 computers: $14,995

"*Millionaire*"-type game built with Quia:

Comes with several customizable templates so you can add in your own content.

Unlimited users: $99

PowerPoint. Creating PowerPoint games can be time-consuming, and thoughtful planning is key, but careful use of hyperlinking can help you design entertaining, engaging games.

Basic PowerPoint games require:

- A title or "start" slide
- A slide with instructions for playing the game
- A slide showing the game board
- Slides for questions and answers

Then:

- Insert hyperlinks

  From questions to answers

  From each answer back to the game board

Then:

- Test, test, test. Check all the links among the slides.
- Once the basic game is completed, save a copy. It can be used as a template for creating future games.
- Go back and add graphics, backgrounds, animations, and other features. Save this complete new game as another file.
- Save everything (slides, sounds, video) in one folder.

Figures 5.15 through 5.17 show sample screens from a *Jeopardy*-type game used in training recently hired employees of a retail electronics store.

A word of caution about creating games like the one shown in Figures 5.15 to 5.17: While it's tempting to copy the format of a popular game show, remember that many elements are copyrighted. I ran across a really nice *Jeopardy*-style game once. Unfortunately, it was called *Jeopardy*, and the designer had actually gone online, found an audio clip of the *Jeopardy* theme song, and embedded it into the game. He'd also included show-specific jargon like "daily double." This designer, probably unintentionally, had crossed the line between borrowing the basics of a familiar format and stealing copyrighted materials.

Although your copy of PowerPoint is a free tool, the Collaborative Learning Systems e-games generator is only $1.80 per game you actually use,

FIGURE 5.15. GAME BOARD FOR POWERPOINT GAME

Digital Cameras	Cell Phones and Pagers	VCRs	DVD Players	Accessories
100	100	100	100	100
200	200	200	200	200
300	300	300	300	300
400	400	400	400	400
500	500	500	500	500

FIGURE 5.16. QUESTION SLIDE FOR "CATEGORY 1 FOR $100"

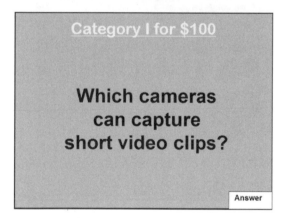

FIGURE 5.17. ANSWER SLIDE

and use of the Quia templates is only $99 (or less) per year. It is less time-consuming to create a game with one of the templates, the finished game will have a smaller file size than PowerPoint, and use of the products will help you steer clear of copyright problems. The Flash products also offer more sophisticated options, such as running timers and scorekeeping, than does Power-Point. If you can find the money, the Flash products will likely give you a higher-quality, lower-labor product. You can always still design your basic course with PowerPoint and insert a hyperlink to the purchased game. Templates for some PowerPoint games are available at http://www.bozarth zone.com. Try also searching the web for "PowerPoint games" and "Creating games in PowerPoint."

SCORECARD

PowerPoint Game

Cost of well-known game show–type software for 200 learners, 1 designer: $4,500

Cost if you already own PowerPoint: $0

In creating quizzes and games, try to provide meaningful feedback, especially for learners who are working alone with a self-directed e-learning program. I once had learners preview an expensive vendor-made e-learning product. The game itself was fine, but the feedback was problematic. Clicking the wrong answer took the learner to a screen with, "That's wrong!" in giant red letters accompanied by a dreadful buzzer noise. The noise was irritating enough to cause learners to quit the game, and the overwhelmingly negative feedback was discouraging. "That's wrong" is less effective than, say, "That's wrong. The correct answer is item C: 164." I recently ran across an online quiz with twenty true-false items on one page (far too many, by the way). I clicked randomly without even reading the questions. The next screen listed the ones I missed, and the final screen said, "Congratulations! You have completed the course!" I hadn't even *read* the information, much less learned it. A good quiz or game will help learners learn or give them some reinforcement for learning.

Excel. Excel's hyperlinking capabilities make it possible to create games similar to those in PowerPoint; in addition, a gifted designer can create fill-in-the-blank activities using Excel spreadsheets. (Templates for this are available at http://www.bozarth zone.com.) Be aware that learners will need Excel in order to use

Try searching the web for:

- Free online game creation tools
- Free game engines
- Create-your-own online games
- Create free Flash games

them. To learn more about the possibilities of using Excel for quizzes and games, try searching the web for "Excel games" and "Creating games in Excel."

Searches: Treasure Hunts and Web Quests

Great free design approaches include search activities such as those described below.

Treasure Hunts

Treasure hunts, also called scavenger hunts, are a great **free** way to teach learners to use reference materials such as manuals, guidebooks, troubleshooting guides, and instruction booklets and to help them learn to navigate online resources like the company intranet. In keeping with the theme of using what you have, the treasure hunt can be an effective tool for maximizing use of existing documents that your organization may already have on its website. Here are some sample treasure hunt assignments:

"Go to our benefits home page: www.ourbenefits.com. Locate the insurance benefits calculator, and use it to determine the monthly fee for fully covering one dependent child."

"Go to our online policy manual: www.ourrules.com. Find the policy on tuition reimbursement. When do approval forms need to be submitted?"

"Visit our site: www.newproducts.digitalcameras.com. Which new cameras have video capability?"

"The repair person calls from the field and says he is getting no read on the charge to the TG775-H unit. Click here for our *Troubleshooting Guide,* and use it to determine the steps in diagnosing the problem."

Figure 5.18 shows part of a treasure hunt developed for a pharmaceutical firm. It's used in training new telephone counselors working with consumers who are considering buying prescription drugs over the Internet. The treasure hunt requires the new employee to explore the company's own site and become familiar with the same information likely accessed by its callers.

FIGURE 5.18. EXAMPLE OF A TREASURE HUNT

Treasure Hunt   **Topic: Internet Prescription Drug Sales**

Clue 1:	Clue 2:
Go to our page <u>Buying prescription drugs online</u> What are two critical issues when counseling callers about purchasing drugs online? Where else can callers locate information about online prescription drug sales?	Many callers will have already accessed the <u>US Department of Commerce</u> website. Go to that site and find the information on this topic. What are the laws regarding importation of prescription drugs? What MUST we caution our callers about?

Web Quests

Another search-type activity is the web quest; like the treasure hunt, it is not a product but a way of structuring an assignment. With a minimum of tools, anyone can create an engaging, thought-provoking web quest at no cost. It's especially good for encouraging independent research and ownership of a topic. Learners must explore assorted sites, evaluate and compile information, and use that information to create a final product.

The designer takes a topic (such as diversity, conflict resolution, new product development, or new sales regions) and identifies tasks that will meet stated learning objectives ("develop knowledge of socioeconomic reality of another culture," "use mediation techniques to resolve conflict successfully," or "develop strategy for marketing in new region"). The web quest concludes with a final product or project. Separate pages describe the roles and processes learners should use, provide resources (preferably online), and define the ways the final product will be evaluated. Web quests can be built with any web page creation tool, including Microsoft Word.

Figures 5.19 through 5.24 show an example of a web quest. This one, on preventing mad cow disease, was created by Leo M. Grassi of Interactworks; the images in the figures are used with his permission. The various screen shots show the purpose of the assignment, the task, the rules, and the evaluation criteria and provide links for additional resources for the participants.

Web quests are good for supporting courses in which some attitudinal change is desired, for instance, diversity training (each team is assigned a different culture) or leadership skills (each team is assigned a particular facet of leadership to research: motivation, mission/vision, ethics, managing problem performers; or given a management theory to research: quality circles, empowered management, situational leadership). A web quest can also serve as a good homework assignment for groups that may otherwise be spending some time together in the classroom—in an ongoing leadership course, for instance.

The repository for much web quest information is at San Diego State University (http://webquest.sdsu.edu) and is full of tutorials, templates, ideas, suggestions, and guidelines. More examples can be found via a web search for "webquest."

FIGURE 5.19. INTRODUCTION PAGE FOR MAD COW WEB QUEST

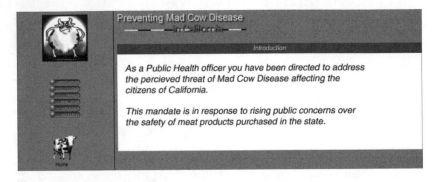

FIGURE 5.20. DESCRIPTION OF THE ASSIGNMENT

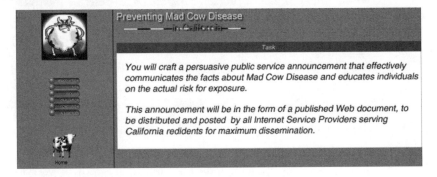

FIGURE 5.21. OUTLINE OF PROCESS TO BE USED

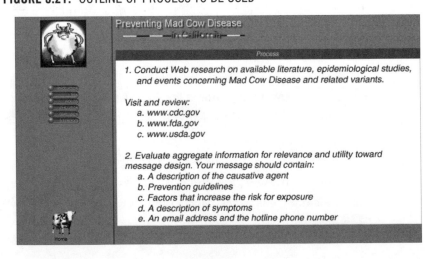

FIGURE 5.22. EVALUATION RUBRIC

Preventing Mad Cow Disease
— — —in California — —

Evaluation

You will be evaluated based on this rubic:

	Developing	Accomplished	Exemplary
Public Service Message	Excessive technical jargon Irrelevant information No hot line or email contact	Moderate technical jargon Adequate message focus	Minimal use of technical jargon Targeted, specific information
Web Page	Page in text-intensive and difficult to read Choice of graphics/metaphor conveys message poorly	Page text quantity is adequate and easy to read Graphics/metaphors reasonably convey message	Page text/page designed for optimal readability Graphics/metaphors convey message in a powerful way

FIGURE 5.23. CONCLUSION AND SUGGESTIONS FOR ADDITIONAL RESOURCES

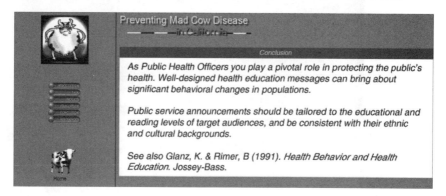

Preventing Mad Cow Disease
— — —in California — —

Conclusion

As Public Health Officers you play a pivotal role in protecting the public's health. Well-designed health education messages can bring about significant behavioral changes in populations.

Public service announcements should be tailored to the educational and reading levels of target audiences, and be consistent with their ethnic and cultural backgrounds.

See also Glanz, K. & Rimer, B (1991). *Health Behavior and Health Education.* Jossey-Bass.

FIGURE 5.24. REFERENCES

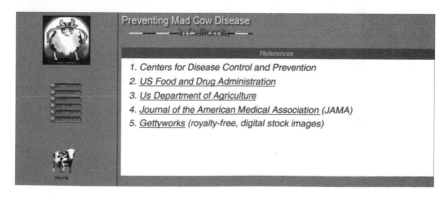

Preventing Mad Cow Disease
— — —in California — —

References

1. Centers for Disease Control and Prevention
2. US Food and Drug Administration
3. Us Department of Agriculture
4. Journal of the American Medical Association (JAMA)
5. Gettyworks (royalty-free, digital stock images)

Puzzles

Puzzles provide still another way of interacting with materials and give learners a break from content-heavy programs. Two common puzzle formats are the crossword and the jigsaw.

Crossword Puzzles

Crossword puzzles are good tools for teaching definitions and terminology. Hot Potatoes has a crossword-creation function; other similar products are available at low or no cost on the web. Figure 5.25 shows a crossword puzzle built with Hot Potatoes.

FIGURE 5.25. EXAMPLE OF A CROSSWORD PUZZLE CREATED WITH HOT POTATOES

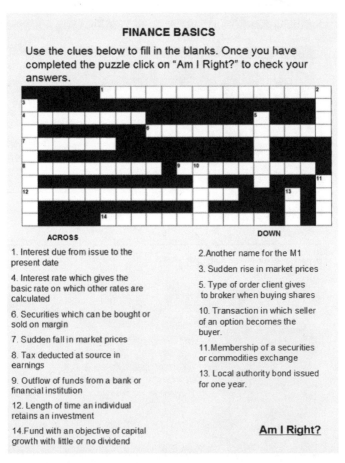

FINANCE BASICS

Use the clues below to fill in the blanks. Once you have completed the puzzle click on "Am I Right?" to check your answers.

ACROSS

1. Interest due from issue to the present date

4. Interest rate which gives the basic rate on which other rates are calculated

6. Securities which can be bought or sold on margin

7. Sudden fall in market prices

8. Tax deducted at source in earnings

9. Outflow of funds from a bank or financial institution

12. Length of time an individual retains an investment

14. Fund with an objective of capital growth with little or no dividend

DOWN

2. Another name for the M1

3. Sudden rise in market prices

5. Type of order client gives to broker when buying shares

10. Transaction in which seller of an option becomes the buyer.

11. Membership of a securities or commodities exchange

13. Local authority bond issued for one year.

Am I Right?

Jigsaw Puzzles

A jigsaw effect can be created with drag-and-drop tools such as those provided with Coursebuilder or with free or inexpensive jigsaw-creation software available on the web. Figure 5.26 shows a puzzle designed to help new employees memorize the store layout; Figure 5.27 shows the completed puzzle. The puzzle was built with Coursebuilder as a drag-and-drop activity.

FIGURE 5.26. SCRAMBLED JIGSAW PUZZLE PIECES

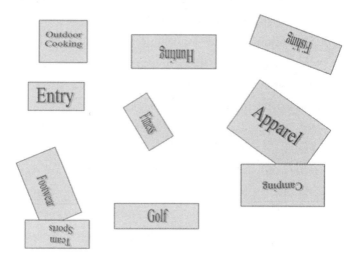

FIGURE 5.27. COMPLETED JIGSAW PUZZLE

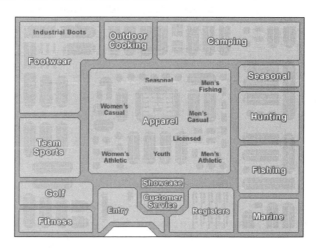

Simulations

Simulations (also called *action mazes*) are an excellent way of providing learners with opportunities to practice skills in a safe environment. A well-constructed simulation shows the learner the consequences of his or her actions and is thus a powerful learning tool.

Simulations are good for tasks involving conversations, such as customer service representatives dealing with an angry caller, sales representatives learning new company lingo or explaining product knowledge, or managers discussing performance with employees. They're also great for leading learners through a decision-making process, like setting priorities or choosing a particular course of action, or for activities that would be dangerous or expensive to practice live.

Among the best-known commercial vendors of simulations is Forio (http://www.forio.com). Forio's Broadcast Express is free, entry-level web simulation software. The product walks you through developing and launching your own simulation and will host one simulation for free (after that, a fee is charged).

You can also build free simple simulations in PowerPoint. Figure 5.28 shows the layout for part of a simulation on choosing good hiring questions. (The text on the slides has been expanded for use in this figure. The live version of this simulation uses audio clips of the interviewee's answers.)

Building a good simulation takes a good deal of planning and patience. Before beginning, be sure to define your objectives: in the case in Figure 5.28, it is to ask interview questions that prompt a thorough answer. You'll likely find it helpful to create a storyboard, diagram, branching flowchart, or other decision-making model to follow.

Another type of simulation doesn't use the branching process so much as present a scenario that participants must then work out. Akin to an elaborate case study, such simulations can be demanding to design but can result in big payoffs. These simulations usually involve materials such as sales orders, work requisitions, e-mails, memos, meeting minutes, reports, and transcripts of phone conversations and may be offered as a blended experience with participants interacting face-to-face in a classroom or by telephone. Learners caught in the heat of the moment tend to want to perform well; giving them realistic scenarios is a powerful motivator.

FIGURE 5.28. PORTION OF A SIMULATION CREATED WITH POWERPOINT

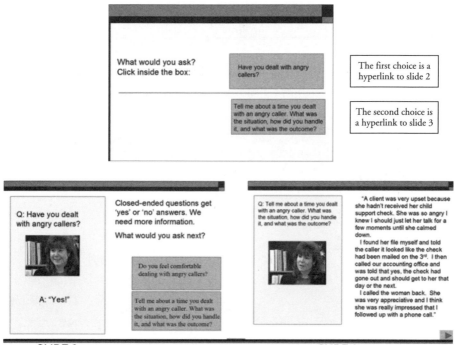

Summary

In creating interesting and engaging activities, the trick is to mix things up. There's an old saying, "If the only tool you have is a hammer, you tend to see every problem as a nail." Once you learn to build an online crossword puzzle or create a slider interaction, you may tend to overuse it. But overreliance on one type of interaction is no better than just showing text on a screen. Keep learning, and keep looking for new tools.

With activities like quizzes and games, it's important to remember that the purpose is not just to entertain. These activities should support learning, encourage application of new knowledge, or in some other way require the learner to have to learn to get the answer.

The best way to learn about designing and using games is to play games. And it's the same with learning about the other exercises described in this chapter. Surfing around on the Internet will give you ideas for content and approaches that might work well for you. Try searching for free online games, quizzes, and other exercises, and every time you see something you like, see if you can figure out how the designer did it—and how you can do it at less cost.

In the next chapter, we'll look at ways collaborative learning activities can encourage participant interaction with material and one another: collaborative learning activities.

Creating Low-Cost Collaboration

COLLABORATIVE STRATEGIES AND TOOLS add interest, facilitate engagement, and build a sense of community. And the great news is that since many collaborative tools are **free** (or almost free), trainers working on tight budgets can use them to build high-quality, high-contact activities such as role plays and interactive case studies.

Synchronous or Asynchronous Collaboration?

There are two approaches to creating collaborative online learning: synchronous, in which people are online together at the same time (as with chat, a live virtual classroom, or a web conference), and asynchronous, in which people may check in and work at different times (as with a discussion board or e-mail relay game.) In deciding whether to use a collaborative strategy, think about what works best for your topic: a short session on assembling a widget probably doesn't require much discussion, but a class on dealing with challenging clients might benefit from a lively synchronous exchange. When choosing a collaborative tool or approach, there are some additional factors to consider. Table 6.1 sets out some of these issues.

No matter which you choose (and you may choose to combine both), someone still must serve as facilitator and moderator. Lively discussions can easily go off-track, and slow asynchronous discussions often need a jump-

TABLE 6.1. COMPARISON OF ASYNCHRONOUS AND SYNCHRONOUS APPROACHES TO COLLABORATION

Asynchronous	Synchronous
Free with tools such as e-mail, discussion boards, and blogs	Some free voice-over-Internet protocol services now available
	Some products offer free chat. For other products, (1) at minimum, costs of conference phone call; (2) if using hosted, full-function web conferencing or virtual classroom tool, up to hundreds of dollars per user per month, generally requiring twelve-month contract
Learners interact with content	Learners interact with each other and content
Time is learner controlled	Learners must adhere to schedule
Text	Talk
No issues with time zones or shift schedules	Scheduling can be complex if learners are in different time zones or working different shifts
Introverts love it	Extroverts love it
	Helps ensure participation in training
	Provides real-time interaction with subject matter experts
	Useful when a group such as a work team dispersed geographically needs to interact at once

start. Even experienced trainers need to practice in order to develop the new skills needed for facilitating interaction online.

We begin by taking a look at synchronous and asynchronous tools and then examine ways of using them to build interaction and collaboration.

Synchronous Tools

Synchronous tools allow everyone to participate simultaneously. This can happen as simply as everyone joining a telephone conference call while viewing the same PowerPoint show, which is a relatively inexpensive option, or as elaborately as a web meeting with whiteboards (a screen on which all participants can simultaneously write or draw), audioconferencing, and virtual breakout rooms, all more expensive possibilities.

Chat

Chat allows a number of people to interact live at once. Many programs include a chat tool, including the **free** Yahoo (http://www.yahoo.com) and MSN (http://www.msn.com) groups. This is an evolving field. Chat used to be entirely text based, but now several programs, including Yahoo Messenger, offer video and voice chat options as well. Video chat requires a web camera, described in the next section.

If you plan to use chat, you'll need to talk with your IT staff or otherwise explore the technology issues. Firewalls can present some obstacles to using chat technology; older computers and operating systems can be temperamental about chat products.

Webcams

Web cameras (webcams, for short) can add an interesting wrinkle to online collaboration. These can be used for instructors to broadcast talking headshots of themselves to students, for the class members to broadcast to one another, or for whole groups to participate in video chat in a chat room that allows supplemental use of webcams. Some providers, such as Yahoo Messenger, offer video chat for **free**. The cost of web cameras is quickly dropping, with a recent newspaper flyer advertising a package of two webcams for $49.

Phone Conferencing

Conference calling provides a good opportunity for learners to hear each other's voices and "humanize" the online experience. It also uses familiar, easily accessible phone technology and circumvents issues with firewalls and bandwidth. Learners new to this approach may need some training in the rules of discussion (for instance, each speaker should identify himself or herself before talking: "This is Mike, and I want to add that . . ."). Providing participants with online visuals they can access while participating in the call (such as a chart on a web page or an online PowerPoint show) can add interest and variety and make the experience more meaningful. The cost of conference calling is determined by what is incurred in terms of long-distance calling charges.

Audioconferencing

Also known as VoIP (voice over Internet protocol), audioconferencing works like a phone conference, but learners speak through a microphone plugged into their computers. The experience is similar to that of the phone conference, although there can be firewall and bandwidth issues. Several vendors offer **free** and low-cost audioconferencing services; try a web search to see what rates and services are available.

Videoconferencing

Videoconferencing, in which groups of people in different locations can interact by video broadcast over the web, is a good technology but can come at a high price in terms of equipment, bandwidth, and human support. You may find inexpensive resources in your community: colleges or large government agencies may have videoconferencing capability they are willing to share or rent. In many training circles, technologies like video chat are beginning to replace traditional videoconferencing.

Web Conferencing and Virtual Classrooms

Good use of web conferencing and virtual classrooms (basically, web conferencing with additional functionality for training applications) can save in travel costs and time away from work. Learners in different locations talk using microphones or typed text chat (or both at once), write on the same whiteboard, and work in groups in different breakout rooms. Although this is one of the more expensive technologies we've looked at in this book, if you have learners or clients in widespread locations or are spending a great deal on conference calls overseas, then the cost of a high-function synchronous learning tool may be a very good investment. Some of the better-known products are Elluminate, Placeware, Centra, vClass, and WebEx.

For basic web conferencing needs, NetMeeting software is included in the MS Office package (versions 98 and higher for **free**). Additional low-cost services are offered by companies such as Placeware ($135 for a two-hour bridge line) and WebEx ($0.45 per minute per user).

The biggest problem with web conferencing is security. The application-sharing capability, such as everyone being able to interact with a whiteboard at the same time, can make a system vulnerable to security breaches. Net-Meeting is **free**, but it brings more security risks than some of the purchased products. Before planning to use one of these products, be sure to talk with IT staff about any security issues.

Skills for the Synchronous Setting

Even seasoned instructors find live online classrooms a bit challenging. You'll need to develop some new skill sets for facilitating live events to keep them lively and interesting. For more information on synchronous training, read Jennifer Hofmann's excellent *The Synchronous Trainer's Survival Guide* (2003) and *Live and Online! Tips, Techniques, and Ready-to-Use Activities for the Virtual Classroom* (2004). Hofmann's company, InSync Training LLC (http://www.insynctraining.com), offers workshops for trainers and provides free orientation sessions for those wishing to try this technology.

Asynchronous Tools

The synchronous versus asynchronous decision, even if money is no object, is analogous to this: Should you visit or call, or will an e-mail do? If it's the latter—that is, people don't need to interact in real time—there are a number of **free** and low-cost tools and approaches to help you encourage interaction among learners. However, with an asynchronous approach, activities may take longer than in the classroom because students will need to figure out how to work together and may need days or weeks to complete assignments.

Blogs

Blogging is a popular new approach and is widely available for **free**. Although blogs (also known as weblogs) were first developed as online journals or diaries, and thus often appear as one person's assorted thoughts and grumblings, they can also serve a group by interest (supervisory skills) or practice (registered nurses) or topic (copyright laws) or assignment ("research and report on our six new products"). Blogs offer limited strategies for organizing content, with messages appearing as a long string in the order in which they are posted. One of the best-known blog sites is http://www.blog.com. Figure 6.1 shows a sample blog page.

An emerging use of the blog is as a substitute for a website; bloggers use the blog as their main page and insert links to other sites.

FIGURE 6.1. EXAMPLE OF A BLOG

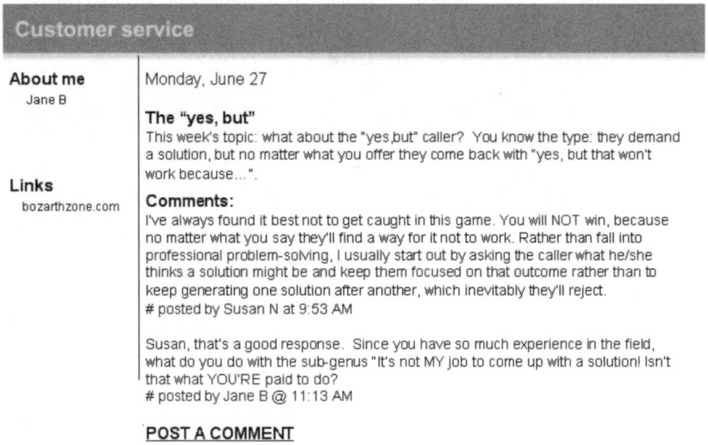

Customer service

About me
Jane B

Links
bozarthzone.com

Monday, June 27

The "yes, but"
This week's topic: what about the "yes,but" caller? You know the type: they demand a solution, but no matter what you offer they come back with "yes, but that won't work because…".

Comments:
I've always found it best not to get caught in this game. You will NOT win, because no matter what you say they'll find a way for it not to work. Rather than fall into professional problem-solving, I usually start out by asking the caller what he/she thinks a solution might be and keep them focused on that outcome rather than to keep generating one solution after another, which inevitably they'll reject.
posted by Susan N at 9:53 AM

Susan, that's a good response. Since you have so much experience in the field, what do you do with the sub-genus "It's not MY job to come up with a solution! Isn't that what YOU'RE paid to do?
posted by Jane B @ 11:13 AM

POST A COMMENT

Discussion Boards

Discussion board software can be downloaded for **free** from many websites (search for "free discussion board") and is included with online community programs such as Yahoo and MSN groups. There's also a popular discussion-only site offered by Voy Forums (http://www.voy.com). Learners access the boards on their own schedules to post their comments and read those of others. Discussion boards allow threaded discussions in which messages are linked by topic.

e-Mail

You and your learners likely already have e-mail; if not, **free** e-mail accounts are available through sources such as Yahoo (yahoo mail) and MSN (hotmail). In addition, e-mail-based discussion listservs are free and can provide support for many training topics. A recent quick web search revealed the existence of more than ten thousand lists, focusing on myriad specific topics. It's also possible to create a listserv for a given group, such as members of one training class.

Polls and Surveys

Online communities such as Yahoo groups come with a polling feature; popular vendors of **free** polls and surveys include http://www.zoomerang.com and www.freeonlinesurveys.com. Surveys and polls are useful for activities such as taking votes and sharing opinions, and can be used to set the stage for debate or divide participants into groups for other activities.

Wikis

Wikis are relatively new **free** tools. Unlike blogs, wikis allow people not only to post their own comments but edit those of others. It's a great tool for knowledge management tasks, projects in which people might edit or update someone else's information, or in cases where information is rapidly changing or needs frequent updating. (For an overview of the Wiki format, visit http://www.Wikipedia.com.) It's a dynamic community-created encyclopedia, always evolving and always fresh.

Creating Collaborative Activities

Creative use of these technologies enables the trainer to recreate many of the activities typically used in the classroom.

Online Conversations

Use the "talk tools" such as message boards, conferencing, chat, and e-mail to:

- Assign group discussion on topics such as pros and cons, advantages and disadvantages, good experiences and bad ones, and best practices and lessons learned.

- Conduct brainstorming sessions.

- Facilitate debates.

- Ask individual learners or groups to summarize readings, discussions, role plays, or other experiences.

- Create asynchronous breakout rooms on a discussion board. Set up several different topic threads or subject headings, and then ask learners to choose the conversations they wish to participate in. For instance, in a class on supervisory skills, learners might choose between discussions on handling the problem performer, retaining the talented performer, or motivating the average performer.

- Have learners interview a subject matter expert or authority. If using asynchronous technologies, learners, working singly or in teams, could each conduct an interview and report back to the whole class. Learners using synchronous technologies could all interview the expert at once.

Icebreakers and Other Introductions

E-mail can be used for simple icebreaker and other introduction activities. Provide participants with a group e-mail list, and ask each to post a message answering the kinds of questions often used in classroom icebreaker activities. For instance, participants can be asked to use e-mail to:

- Introduce themselves and provide some personal information.

- Answer questions such as, "What is your favorite hobby [or place or movie]?" "If you were stranded on a desert island, which three books or CDs would you want to have with you?" "If you could invite any three people in all of history to a dinner party, who would you invite, and why?"

- Present a metaphor that represents their job, their future, or their place in the organization, for example.

A fun means of having participants introduce themselves, a good first step toward establishing community among course participants and a substitute for the classroom icebreaker activity, is through the use of student home pages. Free online community tools such as Yahoo! groups give members the option of creating home pages. (These could also be created as Word documents, e-mailed to the instructor, and uploaded as web pages.) They're an excellent way for members who may not otherwise meet to get to know one another and for encouraging learners to try out technology. To create a safe learning environment, make sure students understand the purpose of the activity: as an icebreaker, not a test of the learner's skill at web design. Students could have some discretion in what to include, such as ages of children, favorite sports teams, and work interests. Because some people are uncomfortable posting personal photos on the web, it might be best not to require them. Figure 6.2 shows an example of a student home page.

FIGURE 6.2. EXAMPLE OF A STUDENT HOME PAGE

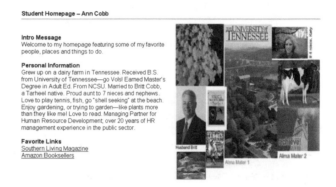

After students view one another's pages, collaboration can be encouraged by setting up asynchronous or synchronous discussions about hobbies, interests, or life experiences or through a quiz based on content from student pages, as shown in Figure 6.3.

FIGURE 6.3. QUIZ BASED ON INFORMATION IN STUDENT HOME PAGES

Question 1   Matching

Pets and hobbies

- Scuba diving
- Has a goat named Stella
- Owns 2 geckos
- Likes to fish with her brother

A. Laura
B. Mary
C. Linda
D. Nicole

Question 2   Matching

Match the person to the info

- Recently joined Weight Watchers
- Favorite book: "To Kill a Mockingbird"
- Youngest of SIXTEEN children!

A. Judith
B. Ann
C. Connie

Question 3   Matching

Who's where?

- Traci
- Gail
- Laura

A. Rural Hall/Winston-Salem
B. Jacksonville
C. New Bern

Team Assignments

Here's an example of an asynchronous threaded discussion used for a team assignment. (This was done using a discussion board but would work quite well by e-mail as well.) Members of an online class were grouped into teams denoted by colors. Figures 6.4 through 6.7 show the Red Team's discussion. The team then discussed how to compile and post their final answer (see Figure 6.8), which Laura submitted. Other groups in the class, working on other assignments, were able to both read and respond to the Red Team's case and also to print and use the criteria list as a future real reference.

FIGURE 6.4. ASSIGNMENT FOR TEAM DISCUSSION

Group Discussion Board - Red

Criteria   [7 messages]
                                                                   [All read]

You are now sophisticated users of online products. What criteria would you use
to evaluate the quality of an e-learning program, either one a vendor was offering
or one you were developing in-house?
If appropriate, refer to specific products we've seen.

By next Wednesday, post your group's consensus response on the main discussion board.

FIGURE 6.5. TEAM MEMBER KAREN'S CONTRIBUTION TO THE TEAM DISCUSSION

Current Forum: Criteria
Date: Mon Nov 4, 2004 3:47 pm
Author: Karen
Subject: Criteria RE Red Team

Hello, Red Team.

Here's a stab at our criteria project.

Assuming I would be working with outside e-learning vendors rather than developing everything in-house, I would:

- Interview vendor candidates and pay special attention to those that spent more time learning about our organization.
- Secure logins and passwords for self and key stakeholders.
- Invite top 2-3 candidates to meet with organization's MIS department.
- Ask for a list of references and speak to former customers.
- Secure agreement for a pilot. Test before buying.
- Final purchase based on how well, how fast and how cost effectively each product met performance objectives, needs of participant population, organization's technical sophistication, and budget. Assess vendor's willingness to "work with" the organization

---

FIGURE 6.6. TEAM MEMBER SUSAN'S THOUGHTS ON THE TEAM DISCUSSION

Current Forum: Criteria
Date: Mon Nov 4, 2004 6:03 pm
Author: Susan
Subject: Criteria RE Red Team

Karen, I agree with most of your steps. I would add:

Interview process: how easy is the administration piece—tracking, setup, customization? Measurement such as pre and post tests?

Learner: ease of use, navigation tools clear and easy to follow? Is learner provided with ongoing feedback? Is course interactive (games, etc) or "wall of words"? Is product supported with off-line activities such as learning lab guidelines or facilitation guides for conference calls? Is there a FAQ or help page?

Technical: Ease of installation. Can it operate on our network? Does it require additional downloads/plugins? Any firewall issues?

Course samples: need to view before scheduling onsite visit—CDs or link to Website for demo courses.

FIGURE 6.7. TEAM MEMBER HENRY'S ADDITIONS TO THE TEAM DISCUSSION

Current Forum: Criteria
Date: Tues Nov 5, 2004 10:17 am
Author: Henry
Subject: Criteria RE Red Team

Hi, Susan and Karen.

I think you've both done a terrific job of describing a solid process for working with vendors. I'd like to add some ideas about what we'd like to see in terms of the PRODUCT versus managing the vendor. I'm thinking of things like good use of graphics, appropriate use of bells and whistles, bookmarking and letting the learner go back to review material, etc.

FIGURE 6.8. RED TEAM'S FINAL CONSENSUS POST

Current Forum: Criteria
Date: Wed Nov 6, 2004 4:33 pm
Author: Laura
Subject: Criteria RE Red Team

Criteria for Evaluating an Online Product:

Compatible with in-house systems
Customizable
Designed according to learning principles
Clear performance goals
Measurement capabilities, including pre and post tests
Ongoing feedback
Easy to navigate
Appealing and engaging, but not distracting
Appealing backgrounds and meaningful graphics
Interactive (games, case studies, simulations, etc.)
Supported by off-line activities like learning labs and conference calls
Allows learner to go back and review units of instruction
Adequate practice opportunities
FAQ or help readily available

Vendor Relationship

Interview potential vendors
Final candidates evaluated against the following criteria:
   Product quality
   Understanding of organization's business
   Past success
   Technical compatibility
   Results of pilot
   Stakeholder feedback
   Vendor's ability/willingness to respond to feedback

This assignment proves that online collaboration is possible and valuable. It also demonstrates the notion that "two heads are better than one," since collectively the group came up with a better response than any one member did singly.

Case Studies

If using a case study activity asynchronously, as with a discussion board, assign a deadline for submitting completed information. Here's a sample case study from Don Clark's "Big Dog" website (http://www.nwlin.com/_donclark/hrd):

Example of an Online Case Study:
Wholesome Path Promises Safety Improvements

Wholesome Path manufactures organic whole grain foods. It started out as a very small company of about ten people. About four years after its conception, its leader, Rebecca Waits, took the small company public. It soon began growing at a very rapid pace. Throughout this high-growth period, it has remained in touch with its all-natural organic roots and the people who work for the company. Although management was good at maintaining its organic and food certifications, they were not very knowledgeable about the many safety regulations that govern manufacturing plants. The company soon found itself in trouble when Occupational Safety and Health Administration (OSHA) inspectors showed up at its doors to perform a federal inspection.

The OSHA inspections were triggered by employee complaints. The chief inspector reported that OSHA's chief concern was to ensure that the workplace is safe for workers.

Worker training and safety programs at Wholesome Path's food processing plant were found to be below industry standards during the inspection. Inspectors identified more than twenty-five safety and health hazards at the plant during a three-month inspection conducted. The agency cited Wholesome Path for:

- Violating requirements for turning off machinery during maintenance and providing safeguards so they cannot be restarted during maintenance

- Critical safety guards missing on moving machine parts

- Incomplete procedures for work performed in confined spaces including tanks and pits

- Missing guardrails and safety harnesses to protect workers from fall

- Lack of training for forklift operators

- Posted safety rules not being enforced or obeyed

Wholesome Path agreed to:

- Pay a $90,000 fine

- Put plant supervisors through approved OSHA safety training courses

- Provide safety training to employees

- Make the workplace safer

Wholesome Path's management is now paying more attention to safety at the plant and is committed to bringing its safety program up to the highest standards within the industry. Roy Robes, a spokesperson for the company, said, "We expect to see some positive results from the changes we are now making. Our employees' well-being is our first concern."

Discussion Questions

1. What role can Wholesome Path's human resource department play in making the workplace safer?

2. What might the company have done to keep from getting into trouble with OSHA?

3. What type of analysis might you perform to ensure that the safety training programs are adequate?

4. What would you recommend if your analysis showed that training was not the answer?

5. What type of training could you provide for the supervisors and management, besides safety, that would help them comply with OSHA requirements?

Role Plays

Role plays can be posted on a website and facilitated using threaded discussions, e-mail, or private group work, or they can be facilitated with one of the synchronous tools. The trainer will need to provide a scenario or problem, assign roles, and give basic information about carrying out activities. The example that follows was done on a discussion board, but it could have been conducted by e-mail too.

Role Play: The Wichita Situation

Scenario: The team is made up of a sales manager, the District 1 Sales Rep, and the District 2 Sales Rep. A new product is about to be released after several false starts and stalls. The client in Wichita is extremely anxious about the delivery of the product and is threatening to cancel her contract if any more delays occur.

Each role player is e-mailed the role play's objectives, instructions for participating, and a description of only his or her own role:

Sales Manager: You are a company veteran and are used to the last-minute chaos of a new product launch. Today you will post a message titled "Product Development" explaining that a last-minute inspection of your new product showed a small flaw that can be easily corrected but will delay shipment for a couple of days.

District 1 Sales Rep: You have been with the company only six months and are frustrated with the organization's bureaucratic approaches and difficulties in simple communication. You have six new prospects clamoring for your new product, which had a promised delivery date of ten days ago. You suspect that your manager is too flexible and fails to be assertive in dealing with production and her manager. You will be participating in an e-mail discussion with your manager, the district 2 sales rep, and an angry client. Please respond in character as you feel is appropriate.

District 2 Sales Rep: You have been with the company for three years and are ready for more responsibility. You want to move into management, and have been told you have a bright future, but this problem in Wichita is threatening to derail your whole career. You must find a way to satisfy this client without causing more problems at the home office. You will be participating in an e-mail discussion with your manager, the district 2 sales rep, and an angry client. Please respond in character as you feel is appropriate.

Angry Client: You will be receiving an e-mail saying there's yet another delay in the product you've been waiting for. You like the company but are tired of the endless communication loops and almost-missed promises. This latest development is the last straw! Post a reply expressing your frustration.

Figure 6.9 shows how the first day's discussion thread looked; messages have been collapsed so only subject headings appear. (Note that learners do not have to be online simultaneously to participate.)

e-Mentoring, e-Coaching, and e-Tutoring

Activities involving e-mentors, e-coaches, and e-tutors can provide valuable reinforcement for training and ongoing development. The difference may be mostly one of semantics, but the generally accepted definitions are that an *e-mentor* is an experienced member of the same field (for example, a veteran supervisor, salesperson, or nurse) who shares knowledge and expertise with a novice; an *e-coach* is someone who helps define goals and build plans for

FIGURE 6.9. DISCUSSION THREAD AT END OF FIRST DAY OF ROLE PLAY

New product development _____ Sales manager
Release Thursday?_____ District 1 rep
Delivery issues _____Demanding client
HOLD ON! _____Sales manager
REVISED specs on new products_____Sales manager
FW: Angry client-Wichita again_____ District 2 rep

development; and an *e-tutor* is someone assigned to work with another person to build a particular ability or skill. Each works individually with a particular learner, and in most cases the two decide on their method of communication: telephone, chat, or e-mail. Note that it is possible for learners in the same course to serve in these roles to support each other.

Storytelling and Story Sharing

Another way of building collaboration and a sense of community is through sharing stories and anecdotes. Figure 6.10 shows an example from a course for new managers, many of whom were struggling with making the transition from employee to manager.

FIGURE 6.10. EXAMPLE OF STORYTELLING

Summary

Thoughtful use of collaborative activities can strengthen the quality of the learning experience and encourage the development of a learning community. In addition, trainers struggling to create quality e-learning experiences with limited resources will find the creative use of the many free and low-cost collaboration tools an excellent way of adding interest and variety to their programs.

So far we've looked at ways of creating basic training programs and enhancing them with free and inexpensive graphic elements, interactive exercises, and strategies for collaboration. In the next chapter, we'll examine ways to support training efforts and enhance workplace performance through the creation of online job aids and other tools.

Creating Performance Support Tools on a Shoestring

E-LEARNING CAN DO MUCH more than just provide training. And it's a good thing, as research shows that 70 percent of workplace learning occurs outside formal classroom instruction (Dobbs, 2000). Consider that over the span of a career, an employee spends many work days punctuated only occasionally by a training event. A new supervisor, for example, might initially attend orientation and then training in specifics of supervisor issues like the agency's recruitment and discipline procedures. He or she will later perhaps participate in some sort of leadership program and finally attend a retirement planning seminar. Figure 7.1 illustrates this pattern.

The spaces between these events are filled with many types of informal learning (see Figure 7.2). The supervisor goes through her days learning through trial and error, talking with other supervisors, conversations with her manager, and maybe self-directed research and reading. For the most part, it is in these spaces that real learning occurs. It may take years and it may not be structured, but the simple law of averages says that much more will be learned outside the classroom than in.

FIGURE 7.1. TYPICAL TRAINING EVENTS IN A CAREER

Source: Used with permission of Bob Mosher.

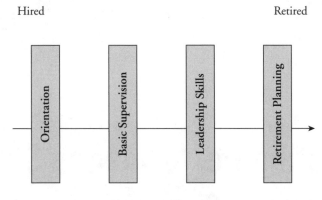

FIGURE 7.2. WHERE REAL LEARNING OCCURS IN A CAREER

Source: Used with permission of Bob Mosher.

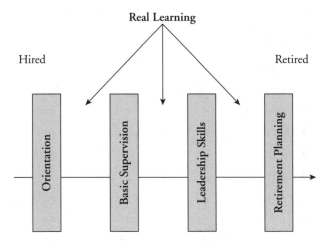

E-learning approaches can help fill in these spaces with performance support, coaching, and collaboration tools. Also called *job aids,* such elements
include checklists, flowcharts, databases, online discussion sites for employees with similar job duties, and reference materials.

In thinking about performance support tools, keep in mind the notion of "bite sized." Many of us in our day-to-day work need an immediate solution to some small problem (How do I set up a conference call? What's the procedure for filing an accident report?) and don't have time to wait until a class on the topic happens to be offered again. Such small pieces of information are ideal candidates for web placement. Even better, they can be created for **free** or at low cost, often from already-haves like Word and PowerPoint, and in many cases they may already exist in the form of user manuals and handouts from training programs. Give some serious thought to ways you can use these inexpensive or free tools to fill in the gaps between training events.

Electronic Performance Support Systems and Workflow Learning

The training and instructional design fields have increasingly expanded to include noninstructional and performance technology solutions. With the rise of easily accessible computer technologies came the idea of the electronic performance support system (EPSS), a computer-based system designed to provide workers with just-in-time tools and other support for work tasks (Reiser, 2001; Wager and McKay, 2002). For those unfamiliar with the EPSS concept, consider this analogy: people wishing to complete their own income tax returns can now simply have the popular TurboTax software walk them through the task rather than attend a two-day tax preparation seminar.

An exciting new next-level development is the emergence of workflow learning. Far beyond the use of simple support tools or even whole electronic performance support systems, workflow learning provides each worker with "just-for-me" tools at the right time. While the EPSS might give all employees access to, for instance, the same software products and company reference materials, workflow learning provides each employee with an individualized "dashboard" of customized job aids and references, relevant to the specific job, on his or her own computer screen. There is no transfer of learning because learning is embedded in the work itself. This holds great promise for those interested in developing e-learning from online training to workplace solutions. Search the web for more information and news about the evolution of workflow learning.

When to Use Performance Support Tools

Amy Corrigan and Eve Drinis of http://www.e-learningguru.com offer ideas for situations appropriate for use of a job aid or performance support tool as outlined in Table 7.1.

TABLE 7.1. SITUATIONS APPROPRIATE FOR USE OF A PERFORMANCE SUPPORT TOOL

Source: Used with permission of Kevin Kruse.

Situation	Examples
Infrequent tasks	Filling out travel expense report; setting up a conference call
Simple but important tasks	Entering a sales order
Tasks that apply to a large population	New version of employee time card system
Tasks that apply to a small population	Instruction for the person and the backup responsible for performing the accounting department's month-end closing
Tasks that apply to a population with a high turnover	Guidelines for note keeping for health care technicians; online tutor for cash register operations
Tasks based on step-by-step procedures	Steps involved in the picking-packing-shipping process
Tasks that require criterion-based decision making	Categorizing items in a ledger

Free Search Tools

Materials such as e-versions of policies, handbooks, and manuals to use as support tools are searchable for **free**. MS Word documents can be searched by clicking "Edit—Find" and then typing a word or phrase into the search box, as shown in Figure 7.3.

FIGURE 7.3. EXAMPLE OF "EDIT—FIND" COMMAND USED
TO SEARCH A WORD DOCUMENT

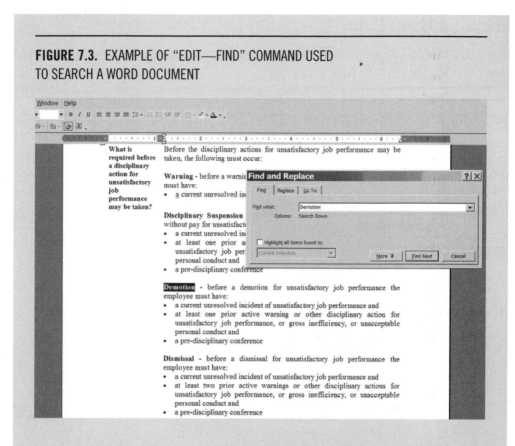

Documents saved in the PDF format can be similarly searched by clicking "Search" and typing the phrase into the box that appears. To help learners search other types of materials, including entire websites, try searching the web for free code that will allow you to insert a search tool.

Which Tool to Use

Table 7.2 provides some guidelines for developing performance support tools.

TABLE 7.2. GUIDELINES FOR CHOOSING A JOB AID

Source: Adapted from material developed by San Diego State University graduate student Erika Lin Beuerlein. Used with permission of San Diego State University/Encyclopedia of Technology Education.

Type	Format	Examples
Step	Sequence, activity, process	Application process How to build a deck Installation manual
Worksheet, calculator	Presents steps Allows calculation or response	Tax form Cost justification Home loan application
Array	Presents large amounts of information Answers who, what, where Useful for frequently changing data	Dictionary Malfunction codes Produce codes at grocery checkout
Decision table	If-then situations Solutions Troubleshooting	Benefits tables Troubleshooting guides Parliamentary procedures guides
Flowchart	Series of yes-no questions Shows decision-making process Results in single decision or action	Chart for determining which statistical formula to use Process for approving policy Receptionist's chart for matching type of call to a department or manager
Checklist	Presents guidelines for optimal performance Lists critical information	Vehicle diagnostic checks List of job application materials Evening closing procedures
Example	Shows finished model to follow	Completed intake forms Sample letter with critical points highlighted Example of finished product

Performance Support Tools: Some Examples

Some examples of job aids are shown in Figures 7.4 through 7.6. Effective job aids include only the information that is truly relevant to completing a given task, are written from the user's point of view, and make the information easy to find. They are also stored or kept on file in a way that makes them quickly accessible.

FIGURE 7.4. SAMPLE WARNING LETTER

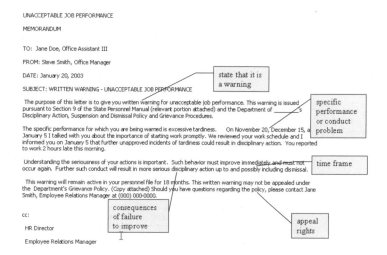

FIGURE 7.5. CALCULATOR USED IN A FARM SUPPLY STORE

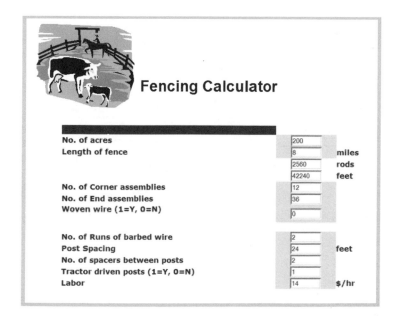

Figure 7.6 shows a performance support tool used by the Internal Revenue Service. Designed to help inexperienced processors handle both walk-in and telephone inquiries, the tool has step-by-step instructions for processing the W-7 form, decision support tools, and links to other references. Designer Suzanne Brown notes that this tool was developed by repurposing existing paper classroom materials.

FIGURE 7.6. PERFORMANCE SUPPORT TOOL USED BY THE INTERNAL REVENUE SERVICE

Source: Used with permission of Suzanne B. Brown.

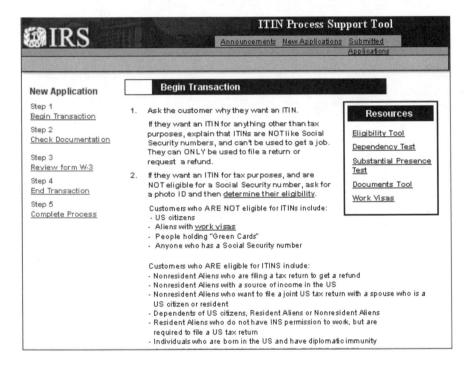

Case Study: Help for Volunteers

NoVa Help is a nonprofit community service agency with one small office supporting a number of field-based workers. The office is staffed largely by volunteers who each work one or two shifts per month. Although they receive initial orientation training, the volunteers do not work often enough to be able—or, in fact, need—to memorize a number of work tasks. NoVa Help's manager developed the tool shown in Figure 7.7 to provide support for these volunteer workers. This is a Word document with hyperlinks to other documents, many of which already existed though were stored in various computer files. The cost to create this tool: $0. In addition, because it needs to be accessed by the worker using the office computer, the page does not need to be accessed over the web. It is stored in the computer's hard drive and easily accessed by clicking an icon on the computer desktop screen.

FIGURE 7.7. PAGE OF PERFORMANCE SUPPORT TOOLS FOR PART-TIME VOLUNTEER STAFF

HELP!! For our Volunteer Staff:

OFFICE EQUIPMENT

Phone
Fax machine
Copier
Printer
Scanner

If you need other help: the user manuals for the office machines are in the third drawer on the left.

REFERENCE MATERIALS

Services list
Community partners contact information
Program outreach information
Referring callers to other agencies

CALLER SITUATIONS

The low literacy caller
The ESL caller: contacting and working with an interpreter
The angry caller
The caller who demands to speak to "someone in charge"

FORMS

Intake
Release
Complaint
Requisition

Carol's cell phone number

Summary

Performance support tools can help provide informal learning, make life easier for employees, and possibly even replace training events (live or online). They can also often be created quickly and easily from products already available to the developer so may be of special interest to training professionals who are working on a shoestring. Additional samples of support tools (for instance, forms with important areas animated in PowerPoint) are available at http://www.bozarthzone.com.

In the next chapter we'll round out our decision to build an e-learning program by leveraging existing resources and sharing expertise.

Leveraging Resources

SOMETIMES BUILDING A QUALITY solution requires something you don't have: money, time, a particular piece of software or equipment. In this chapter, we'll look at some creative means of obtaining solutions through sharing, networking, bartering, and finding inexpensive or even free help. We'll also look at another valuable means of leveraging resources: reusing the e-learning materials you create.

Sharing

If during your web-surfing sessions you happen across a perfect graphic, an especially well-written explanation, or an animation of a process very similar to your own, contact the site's webmaster and ask if you can use it. If you are with a nonprofit organization or otherwise not positioned to gain income from such use, you might be surprised at how willing others are to let you use their products. Most people want to see their work used. Promise to give credit, offer effusive thanks, and see what you get.

The Spirit of Sharing

The online language program created with Hot Potatoes shown in Figure 5.8 was developed by England's Ashcombe School, which makes its products available for free on the web (http://www.ashcombe.surrey.sch.uk/Curriculum/modlang/videos.htm). This e-mail from Ashcombe webmaster David Seume is a testament to the spirit of sharing resources:

Dear Jane,

On behalf of The Ashcombe School, I give permission for you to cite our contribution to the pool of e-learning resources and to use screen shots as you see fit.

I should explain that, as a specialist language college (although also a regular state secondary school) under the aegis of the Department for Education and Skills' Specialist Schools Trust, The Ashcombe fulfils its remit to share "home-grown" resources with others; hence the fact that you have found them openly and freely available on the Internet.

Incidentally, we know from our web statistics that a large number of schools in the UK and overseas regularly access these video materials. It helps make the effort and commitment feel worthwhile.

Good luck with the book!

David Seume
ICT Adviser/Webmaster
The Ashcombe School
Surrey, England

You can link to other sites without violating a copyright. You cannot, however, copy something from a site and put it on your own product without permission. Once, for instance, I wanted to use a particular film clip from a big-budget studio movie. I couldn't afford rights to the clip, but the studio had the clip on its own site. Legally I couldn't download the clip and embed it in my own program, so I got permission from the studio to link to its site and then on my own page. I instructed learners to go to the studio site, view the clip, and return to my lesson.

Be careful about the sites you link to. Communicate with the site owner to make sure it's all right to link to the site and to ascertain the safety of the link.

Case Study: Sharing and ZEF

The Centre for Distance Education (ZEF), housed at Germany's Carl von Ossietzky University of Oldenburg, has engaged in a number of cooperative projects in an effort to cut the costs of academic distance learning. Distance and e-learning Oldenburg faculty members Ulrich Bernath and Thomas Hulsmann (2004) note that ZEF's successful win-win projects have included the following:

• Partnering with the University of Maryland Institute for Distance Education and the University of Maryland University College to implement a worldwide accessible virtual seminar program. Initially meant to provide development opportunities for distance education experts, the project eventually grew into a master of distance education degree program, offered entirely online, which also included the School of Education at Oldenburg University. According to the faculty reporting on the project, "Neither university would have been able to develop and offer such a program on its own" (p. 4).

• Creating a shared ownership arrangement. Using grants and other third-party funds, ZEF, in collaboration with the distance learning and computing centers at the universities in Luneburg and Hildesheim, set up its own Lotus-based learning management system and content management system to create a sustainable infrastructure for managing distance learning. None of the three centers would "have been able to develop and maintain a technical infrastructure of comparable capacity" (p. 5) on its own.

• Franchising. ZEF helped develop a professional nursing certification program. Development costs were 50,000 euros (about $38,000 at the time); spread over 1,260 students, this cost amounted to 40 euros per student. Participating institutions were then charged 50 euros per student they enrolled. Had this project been restricted to the University of Oldenburg, cost per student would have been 250 euros.

In conclusion, Bernath and Hulsmann say, "Our aim is to encourage the exploration of possible synergies and construct mutually beneficial alliances. By doing so there is evidence that high outcomes at low costs can be achieved" (p. 6).

My initial experience with buying e-learning was made possible by the willingness of several agencies to share licenses for a product. Do you have colleagues in straits similar to yours? Does each of you really need your own digital video camera? See if you can find a way to share resources, ideas, and even final products.

Case Study: A True Story About Sharing

Despite their rivalry on the football field, the University of Akron and Kent State University have joined technology forces to maximize e-learning dollars (Gaylord and Tolliver, 2003). With campuses located close together, the schools realized that pooling resources could eliminate duplication of effort, personnel, and services. They developed their shared services model, first by offering online courses in their joint nursing program. They then installed a high-speed fiber-optic line to connect their IT systems, which offered ultra-fast connection speed and shared network applications. They also agreed to share a version of the WEB-CT course platform.

Networking

Often those struggling with costs know the value of sharing knowledge, tools, and resources. My own large community of practice has, in the space of a single week, bailed me out of a sudden need for a Flash designer, gotten three-quarter-inch videotape converted to VHS, and allowed me to offer a full-scale web collaboration meeting for free.

To develop a network, make friends in your local training and web design community. Join local chapters of the American Society for Training and Development (http://www.astd.org) and the International Society for Performance Improvement (http://www.ispi.org). Those in government will find additional support with the National Association for Government Training and Development (http://www.nagtad.org). An excellent national web-based resource is the e-Learning Guild (http://www.elearningguild.com), which offers extensive resources such as white papers, workshops, and discussion boards.

Among the most resourceful people are public school teachers. Thanks to them, we have galleries of sample quizzes built with Hot Potatoes, sites with free templates for PowerPoint games, and approaches like web quests. They know they will never have surplus funds; their willingness to share examples of their ideas and showcase their finished products is invaluable to those of us seeking to create interesting e-learning on limited budgets. Search the web for school- and other education-related sites; make friends with some like-minded teachers; and as much as possible share what you learn and develop.

Bartering

Earlier in the book, you were asked to take inventory of what you already have. A good question to ask now might be, "What do I have to trade?" Can you swap your live stress management workshop for the half-day use of a videoconferencing room? Is a colleague willing to trade use of a digital camera for some time with your DVD burner? I often teach live online classes for free to a virtual classroom community with the agreement that some of my organization's employees can attend at no charge. Bartering services and equipment can result in win-win situations for you and your colleagues.

Inexpensive—and Possibly Free—Help

A colleague, thinking her fourteen-year-old son would need help with a school report, instead found him putting the finishing touches on a Power-Point show complete with animated text, narration, and sound effects. Let's face it: our kids may be better at this than we are and may learn it more easily than we can.

In looking for help with whole programs or perhaps just one small animation or web page, check with local universities, community colleges, technical training schools, and even high schools. You may be surprised at the resources that exist. Many academic institutions offer courses on everything from training and development, to graphic arts and web design, to all manner of computer skills—and instructors are often grateful for real-world projects for students. Establishing a partnership with a program or instructor could pay off in years of mutually beneficial projects. Be very clear about your expectations and deliverables, and be prepared to meet with the students several times. The best thing about working with students is that the project *will* be completed by the end of the semester.

The younger the student is, the more supervision you will likely need to provide. High school students probably need more oversight than graduate students. Factor in the complexity and length of the project, as well as your willingness and ability to supervise, communicate, and manage the project. Chapter Nine offers information on communicating about and contracting for services; treat the relationship with students like any business endeavor, but keep in mind that they are students and often they are young.

For confirmation of the ability of students, try a web search for "student projects + web design." You'll find sites such as Texas State University's list of sample student technology projects. Students in the technical communications program completed projects for clients such as the Academy of Oriental Medicine at Austin; Holt, Rinehart and Winston publishers; and the Susan G. Komen Breast Cancer Foundation.

As an alternative to looking for students in need of projects, check into signing on an intern, either paid or unpaid. As with the other students, interns are looking for experience and items for a résumé.

Repurposing and Reusing

One of the best ways to save money in developing e-learning is to recycle what you have and develop with an eye toward reusing material in the future. It's possible, for instance, to convert paper-based classroom materials to electronic formats and to repurpose existing videotapes into usable online clips. The advent of e-learning has introduced a new concept into training and education: reusable learning objects. Learning objects are small, recyclable pieces of content—for example, graphics, templates, and logos—or bigger pieces of learning content, like a flowchart of a process, a summary of a policy, or a movie clip showing the assembly procedure for a particular product. Basically, a learning object is a piece of content that can be saved and reused.

SCORM

The acronym SCORM frequently comes up in discussions of learning objects. Developed by the U.S. Department of Defense, SCORM stands for "shareable content object reference model." Developing content according to standards means that an item developed for use in a Dreamweaver page last year can be located and reused in a Flash movie next year. It means that an interactive quiz developed by Company X can be shared with Company Y. Working with a vendor that abides by SCORM standards means you can buy an off-the-shelf product and be confident that it will run on your learning management system (if you have one). It means that if you ever purchase or create a formal learning content management system, objects stored there can be found, chosen, and reassembled into a variety of working e-learning modules without your having to recreate the objects so they will work in the newly purchased system.

Conforming to SCORM standards can be a big time- and cost-saver, but its value depends largely on the needs of your organization and the envisioned future of your e-learning program. Companies creating e-learning content for short-term or one-time use, or creating mostly documents that will be stored and deployed in-house (rather than on the web), may manage quite well by developing their own products in their own ways and storing them in a "home-made" library. (This is, in fact, the way much e-learning is developed now.) Companies envisioning longer-term or larger-scale e-learning programs may want to consider moving to a standards-based model of content development. Information on SCORM, including conformance guidelines, is available on the website of the Advanced Distributed Learning Initiative (http://www.adlnet.org) sponsored by the U.S. Secretary of Defense.

A thoughtful, well-catalogued, robust library of reusable objects can create the ultimate learning experience for the learner: the build-it-yourself work product. Suppose a manager wanted to create a module on safety in her work unit, a white-collar office environment. She could choose a video clip on fire extinguisher use, guidelines for using kitchen appliances, and an animated map of the building's evacuation routes and assemble them into a complete training program custom-fitted to the situation of her staff. Another manager in the same organization, but who oversees a production floor area, might add reminders about basic first aid, statistics on injuries in the work unit for the past year, and a video on lifting. The organization could thus offer a good package of just-in-time, just-for-me training opportunities. (In addition, this situation gives the supervisor a vested interest in supporting the training, often a struggle for those in training jobs.)

On the subject of learning objects, here's a great explanation of both objects and a means of cataloguing them (also referred to as *metadata*) from the November 2002 issue of *Sidebars,* an online publication of the British Columbia Institute of Technology (http://online.bcit.ca/sidebars/02november/inside-out-1.htm):

> The basic structure of a learning object can be divided into two main parts: the learning object itself, and the metatag information or metadata that explains what the learning object is. British Columbia's Institute of Technology's Griff Richards once used the example of an exhibit in the Royal British Museum of Archaeology to explain how metadata adds value to a learning object. While touring the museum one day, he saw an exhibit of a piece of granite from an ancient ruin. He knew it was from an ancient ruin because of a small index card placed at the base of the piece of granite. Without that card, the exhibit was just a big rock. It was the index card that gave meaning to the object.
>
> The structure of a learning object is like the exhibit in the Royal British Museum. The content is like the piece of granite, and the metadata is like the index card. The metadata describes the object and places it in context. To continue the analogy, you could take that piece of granite, ship it to the Royal British Mining museum, say, and place a new index card at its base with a description from a mining perspective. You have the same piece of granite, but an entirely different context and a different meaning [Millar, 2004].

Case Study: The Flash Fix

An online course I created needed video clips of performance coaching sessions. We did own the video, which I converted into clips with Windows MovieMaker. We kept running into problems, though, with getting the program to our far-flung learners, first with the server and then with getting media player plug-ins installed on the learner machines. Embedding the video clips into the Flash format seemed a good solution and fit with our future plans to incorporate video into additional programs. I called a friend, Flash whiz Jim Gray, for help (http://www.jfgray.org).

Jim's original plan was, as a favor, to teach me how to take my video clips and create my own Flash movies, but it quickly became apparent that the learning curve for this would be long. In addition, it was the sort of thing I would need only sporadically, meaning that I probably wouldn't remember how to do it the next time and would have to go to Jim again.

Together we created a fairly generic (that is, reusable) template into which video clips I created in MovieMaker could be imported into Flash. Now, when I need to create a video for online use, I pull up the template, delete the old clip, import a new one, and embed the new Flash file in a web page.

The time to develop the template was about an hour. The result was the ability to create unlimited Flash video clips. The cost: $0.

In developing new e-learning programs, don't forget a valuable resource: existing training materials. Perhaps a handout from a classroom workshop can be reused in a new e-learning program, and a calculator tool used in an e-learning program adapted for use as a performance support tool. In working to develop e-learning on a shoestring, try to work with future reuse in mind. It can save a good deal in terms of time, energy, and money.

Summary

Sometimes you don't have to build or buy it yourself. You can beg, borrow, barter, swap, share, collaborate, network, and support local academic endeavors to bring your e-learning projects to fruition, and reuse, repurpose, and recycle your solutions time and again. Creativity and resourcefulness can bring big payoffs.

We've now explored many options in developing our own e-learning solutions in-house. In Part Two, we move to another option: paying someone else to build solutions for you.

Part Two

Buying Your Solutions

9

Paying Someone Else to Build for You

N THIS CHAPTER, WE'LL TAKE a look at building custom content by outsourcing the project, or pieces of it, to a vendor. This path is fraught with potentially expensive mistakes, so we'll cover the essentials of pricing, the issues that affect costs, some negotiation strategies, and tips for special red flags to watch for. Outsourcing development is a complex, potentially lengthy process. Use the information here to help in cutting costs and negotiating effectively, but before you enter into any contractual agreements, spend some time researching all the issues. I strongly encourage you to consult resources such as Patti Shank and Amy Sitze's *Making Sense of Online Learning* (2004) and Kevin Kruse's excellent site, http://www.e-learningguru.com.

Although you are reading this book in an effort to minimize costs, try to keep in mind the real expense of learning as you go. If, when you start, you need to learn everything from the basics of web design to particular authoring

Special thanks to Kevin Kruse, the e-learning guru of http://www.e-learningguru.com and coauthor of *Technology-Based Training* (Keil and Kruse, 2000), for his help with this chapter.

tools and strategies for creating interactive exercises, it may take a very long time to get up to speed. If you're in a hurry for a product, it will probably be cheaper in the long run to pay to outsource the project: there's no learning curve, and your supplier will have a depth of experience it will take a while for you to build. In addition, working with a developer will give you the opportunity to see how it's done so can help you get a clearer picture on how to proceed with your own design projects later.

What Are You Buying?

What's the deliverable? A finished online product? A CD with video clips on it? Be very clear about what you're buying and what you expect to be given at contract's end. You can save some money by outsourcing the "part" rather than the "whole" of your project. Do you need a whole program created from scratch, or do you just need a graphic artist to create some images? If you are in need of multimedia, is it possible that you could create the text for the course and then outsource development of the narration and other media? Depending on the capabilities you have in-house, you might end up sub-contracting many pieces of work (as is common now in the construction industry). Nevertheless, although you may be saving something in cash, you will be encumbering a great deal of your time: the more you have to juggle pieces of a project, the more of your own time you'll have to invest.

How Much Does It Cost?

There are a number of ways an outsourced project can be priced. Some vendors charge by the number of pages or screens. Prices here average about $100 per finished page of text to $200 per page that includes multimedia. Be careful of contracting a price based on number of screens: you may end up with a supplier who says you need fifty when you need only thirty, or may pay for thirty to find out you need twenty more, at additional cost. The finished product should meet the learning objectives, so unless you have already laid out a screen-by-screen storyboard to take to the developer, this figure can be hard to pin down at project outset.

Another option is per-hour pricing. *Hour* is defined as a completed hour of course time, that is, the amount of instruction an average user could complete in one hour. The current price for an hour of content (including some interactive quiz questions, with you providing content, graphics, and media) is around $10,000. Adding in interactivity like drag-and-drop interactions, narration, or multimedia runs $20,000 to $45,000 per hour, and highly interactive programs with simulations are in the neighborhood of $50,000 per hour. The same warnings for pricing by the hour apply here as with the per-screen pricing model.

Still another—and often the best—choice is the project or fixed-bid price. Those who are cost-minded should look for vendors that offer a fixed-price structure for the project. This not only eliminates the possibility of runaway costs but indicates that the vendor is experienced and confident about what he or she is able to provide.

Tough economic times have forced some suppliers to come up with more creative pricing models. Read the fine print to make sure the deal being offered is the one you want. I recently found a site advertising twenty-five "free" pages of course development, including navigation and hosting (you provide all graphics and multimedia). The catch: hosting is $500 per *month*, plus $20 per month per learner.

What Affects Costs?

"Custom development" is not necessarily an expensive undertaking. A number of factors can affect costs:

- Delays, including those caused by changes and indecision on the part of the client
- Multimedia creation and production
- Custom video
- Simulations
- Bookmarking
- Reporting of test scores

- Amount of media
- Stock versus custom graphics, animations, other media
- Custom games

The best way to save money when oursourcing design work:

GET YOUR ACT TOGETHER.

Every time the vendor has to call you, look for something, or wait for you to locate a graphic or something else, it costs you time and, likely, money. Before starting work, provide the vendor with items such as these:

- Photos of your CEO and other staff
- Company logo
- Facility maps and directions
- Company office, telephone, and e-mail directory
- Working links to company websites or other information
- Copies of relevant policies
- Copies of print materials (for example, brochures and catalogues)
- Reference materials
- Company history
- Mission and vision statements

Beyond all that, the vendor needs to know:

- Your learning performance objectives and goals for this program
- Specifics about your expectations
- Specifics regarding how the finished product will look and work (for instance, many universities require the use of school colors somewhere on every web page)
- Information about the type of work your organization performs
- Information about your learners: Who are they? Average age? Education level? Experience with technology?

The clearer you are about what you want and the more specific the information that you provide the supplier, the more likely it is that the project will remain on schedule and within projected costs.

How to Save on Costs

Some developers offer a price cut for development in exchange for ownership of the finished content and source code. Basically, you agree to buy the finished program for which you contracted (at a much lower price), but the vendor can also now sell it to others. This arrangement will save you money, but it can be a high price to pay. When you hand over these rights, you are putting yourself in a vulnerable position. You won't, for instance, ever be able to revise or update your own program. The code and content belong to the vendor, so any future changes will have to be done there. Before signing this away, be sure the final product is the only one you'll ever want—or be prepared to pay for additional costs later. And keep in mind that you don't know what those future costs might be. Furthermore, in regard to content, the vendor will be able to repackage, resell, change, or otherwise do anything else it wants with your material. I probably wouldn't care if a vendor resold my information on the Family Medical Leave Act. But I would mind a vendor remarketing the online version of the workshop I offer based on this book.

Other cost-cutting opportunities exist within the terms of the contract. It should include provisions for program updates and other follow-up issues. Insist on hourly rates for such back-end activities as updates and revisions (currently averaging $100 to $175 per hour). Don't agree to flat rates, fixed prices, or percentages here. Many times a change is nothing more than swapping the previous CEO's photo for the new one. A flat fee of $1,000 per change will make that an expensive graphic swap. Be sure, too, that the contract includes a nonperformance clause so you can recoup expenditures should the vendor fail to complete the project.

An essential part of controlling costs is managing scope creep. I was once involved in purchasing a custom-built course with a team that had agreed at the outset on the size and specifics of the final product. The team project manager worked closely with the vendor to communicate goals and expectations clearly, monitored deadlines, and otherwise worked diligently to keep the project on track. When the vendor came to demonstrate the prototype to the team, the following comments were heard around the table:

"You know, we're going to need to train the engineers eventually too. Can we go ahead and add on a little piece for them at the end?"

"Hey! I like the little Flash movie! Wouldn't it be cool if we could do another one and . . ."

"Could you change the font from Arial to Times New Roman? I know it seems trivial, but it really matters to me."

"I know we only asked for twelve copies but we might as well go ahead and . . ."

Scope creep can cost a bundle in add-ons, changes, revisions, and projects never completed. And note that in this situation, it was not the vendor running up the costs but members of the client team who had set the original goals. Be very clear about the scope of the project, the absolute outcomes, and the drop-dead deadlines before you even begin.

Before embarking on a project, it's important that you hone your project management skills. As the person responsible for outsourcing this project, you will need to establish a schedule for communicating with the vendor. You'll also need to set project milestones. Make expectations and deadlines very clear. Then stick with your strategy. Great project plans frequently run into trouble and costs escalate because no one is monitoring progress or because those doing the monitoring didn't understand the project in the first place.

Beware of Hidden Costs

Some vendors charge for *everything*—every phone call, every page of every fax, every stamp. Be clear on what you will be charged for, and watch out for padding. To save on these kinds of expenses, you might want to give the developer a $20 prepaid phone calling card and do the copying yourself.

Also, be careful of suppliers who develop e-learning with their own proprietary software programs. Some vendors use their own languages, software engines, or other self-built tools. This means you will be forever chained to that vendor and out of luck if the vendor goes out of business. As e-learning guru Kevin Kruse notes, "Your initial investment will be worthless if it needs to be updated and can't be altered." Do your homework, and be sure your vendor is using a standard product like Dreamweaver or Authorware.

Watch out, too, for vendors willing to create "shovelware": you give them a hundred pages of text, and they dump it into a template and call it "e-learning." The vendor should provide a learning experience, not a bunch of text-heavy web pages.

Finally, be wary of the company that has four employees and yet says it can handle everything from creating a custom LCMS to real-time multimedia simulations. Everyone there is either remarkably energetic, not quite truthful, or in fact outsourcing your job. There is nothing wrong with outsourcing services; for instance, not everyone needs a full-time in-house Flash game wizard. But the vendor you're hiring may have little control over that person, so there is a chance your project could be delayed or derailed. Finally, does it matter that you may not know who is looking at your content? If it's proprietary, could be of interest to a competitor, or is in some way secure, you may want to consider whether this vendor is right for you regardless of cost.

Doing Business: The Bid and Request for Proposal Process

Your ultimate goal should be to develop good working relationships with several vendors you can call as needs emerge. Initially, though, you will likely need to go through the process of asking vendors to bid on your project, known as asking for a request for proposal (RFP). Creating a proposal is a considerable task for the vendor, so don't ask for proposals you don't really need, don't ask for proposals because you "want to see what they come up with," and don't ask for proposals because you feel it's the supplier's job to submit them. Vendors will factor the cost of the proposal somewhere in their calculation of the final cost; you will ultimately pay for it.

Case Study: RFP for Online Course

Here's an overview of the bid review process for a recent grant-funded project:

The need: Brief introductory legal compliance training for new staff, meant to fill a gap until the new employees could get to classroom training.

Buy or build? With something in the neighborhood of half a million users and information specific to state regulations, purchasing the product could be justified. The criteria: customized content, the ability to track completion and query information regarding learners, access for up to 500,000 users, and support for learners (for example, issuing passwords, troubleshooting log-in) 24/7 for two years.

Eleven bids were received. Two didn't even mention the query issue; one just sent a price list with nothing else. That alone said something about the quality of these vendors and their commitment to the project. The bids fell between $14,500 and $2.5 million, with most in the $150,000 range. In the case of both the highest and lowest bids, it appeared that the vendors hadn't really read the proposal. The vendor submitting the $2.5 million bid priced out 24/7 tech support far beyond just helping the occasional learner troubleshoot problems logging in. The cheapest bid didn't include licensing for the half-million users. Product demos on the remaining midprice products proved to be the tie-breaker for the final purchase.

Your Best Cost-Saving Strategy: Educate Yourself

A secondary goal of this book is to help you understand some of the magic behind technology. Although you don't need to learn advanced programming skills, understanding the basics of how web design is done will help you become more competent and confident in dealing with vendors and making decisions about how your e-learning money is spent.

For instance, we looked earlier at the availability of some **free** tools, including templates for designing web pages. I recently heard from a vendor advertising the following e-learning development services: you provide all the content, and they put it into a template for you. The cost of pasting your content onto that template? Fourteen *thousand* dollars. Being knowledgeable about e-learning development can help you distinguish a good deal from a bad one and can help you maximize use of your limited resources.

Choosing a Vendor for Developing Custom Content

It's important for you to develop the criteria you want the vendor to meet and then hold him or her to that. Table 9.1 provides some questions to consider when choosing a custom developer.

TABLE 9.1. OUTSOURCING DEVELOPMENT: CHOOSING A VENDOR

	Project management
	Can the vendor describe the process it uses, step by step? Can the vendor document its own business processes?
	What is the vendor's particular expertise?
	What is the vendor's willingness to include you? Will the vendor work from text you wrote, or insist on developing everything its way?
	What is the procedure for managing projects? What mechanisms or people are in place to keep projects on track and on time?
	Who is responsible or accountable? Where does the buck stop?
	How will the final product be evaluated?
	What will you have access to? Can you see storyboards, or will you have to wait for a prototype?
	Will the vendor be available after the product is finished? Do you need the vendor to provide training in using the product?
	Communication and access to people
	How and when will communication take place? Will you have weekly updates by e-mail? Monthly face-to-face meetings?
	Will you be able to meet other people on the team? Are you able to access more than just the sales rep? Can you talk to the designers and programmers?
	Does the vendor outsource these services? Where is the designer?
	How many people have access to your information?
	Contract
	Does the vendor offer fixed per-project prices?
	Who has ownership of content and products? For what period of time?
	Does the contract have a nonperformance clause?
	If possible, is there also a money-back guarantee?
	Do you need security? Will the vendor be dealing with sensitive information?

TABLE 9.1. OUTSOURCING DEVELOPMENT: CHOOSING A VENDOR *(continued)*

	Is there an allowance for tests, pilots, and reasonable changes?
	Product
	What tools does the vendor use? How flexible is the vendor on this point? (Remember that you want a vendor who can create what you need. Do not get talked into changing what you need in order to fit the tool the vendor likes.)
	Look at samples. Are the products text heavy? Is there good, meaningful interaction, or just clicking?
	Can the vendor produce additional products like support tools, references, and study aids?
	Gut-feeling issues
	When you call, does a person always answer, or are you always put into voice mail? How quickly are calls returned?
	Do things seem to be under control, or is there always a feeling of chaos?
	How long has the vendor been in business? How big is the company?
	How was the quality of the proposal? Did the vendor provide the information you requested? (The vendor you choose should be able to follow instructions.)
	References
	Call beyond the first three references, which will likely represent the company's biggest successes.
	Did clients find the vendor and staff generally calm and focused? How did the vendor react to problems, changes, general chaos?
	Were deadlines met? Was the project completed within budget?
	Was the vendor responsive to calls and requests?
	Is the vendor experienced with different types of clients and user groups? (Developing training for medical doctors may not prepare a vendor to develop for food service workers, for example.)
	Is the company stable? Does there seem to be excessive turnover?
	If you feel you aren't getting much information from references, try asking about the vendor's strengths. We live in a litigious age, and people may hesitate to give negative feedback. Ask the reference about the vendor's strengths and talents, what the client liked about the relationship, and whom the client enjoyed dealing with. Hesitation here should send up a big red flag.
	Did the vendor accept responsibility and maintain accountability?

Summary

Before approaching an outside developer or designer, do as much as you can to get your materials and thoughts in order. Know what you can do yourself and what you need to outsource, and don't outsource until you are very clear about your needs and objectives. Get educated about the process: read up on asking for and reviewing RFPs, and develop or find tools for managing communication, projects, and expectations.

In this chapter, we examined the option of outsourcing part or all of a custom development project. Let's move on now to another choice: purchasing a ready-made completed program.

10

Buying Off-the-Shelf Courses

S OMETIMES, EVEN IN THE FACE OF meager funds, it makes more sense to try to find the means of buying an off-the-shelf (OTS) product. Vendors offer quality courses, often with built-in registration, quizzes, tracking, and bookmarking capability—things that can be difficult to build and may otherwise require installation of an in-house LMS. Too, many good online basic skills and soft skills programs already exist, and in many cases are better than anything you could create. Think carefully about, for instance, building an online program on stress management, customer service, or defensive driving techniques. Odds are that someone else has already done a good job of it. In addition, purchasing OTS products can help avoid legal problems because most vendors have legal counsel review products, advise on content, and create any necessary disclaimers. And costs may be lower than you think: as the e-learning field matures, many vendors are moving toward much more flexible pricing models. For example, some have dropped their old requirement for minimum purchases, and others have adopted a pay-as-you-go (rather than up-front purchase) billing approach.

In this chapter, we revisit the buy-versus-build decision, look at some simple cost-cutting techniques and negotiation strategies, and discuss ways of building a good vendor-client relationship. As discussed in Chapter Nine, the decision to make a big outlay of cash or enter into a long-term contract is multifaceted and has much room for missteps. Visit lots of vendor websites, view the course demos each vendor offers, and read up on all the issues at hand before making any decisions.

Déjà Vu: Buy or Build?

In approaching e-learning, you have a choice: buy a ready-made product or build it yourself. Although those with little money may think that hiring a vendor is out of the question, consider the real cost of doing it yourself: your time and salary. If there's any chance at all of finding money, you may want to make a case for outsourcing development or using a purchased product.

In making this decision, consider how many people will use the product. It doesn't make sense to spend 300 person-hours creating an hour-long e-learning program that only 15 people will use. Unless the information is proprietary, absolutely requires company-specific language or graphics, *and* will be used by more than 500 learners, then working with a vendor will likely be your truly less expensive choice.

Know Your Criteria

Before approaching a vendor, be clear on your criteria, and create a list from which to work. It's vital that the OTS product closely match your learning objectives. Courses should also tie to your organization's culture and practice and be appropriate (neither too simplistic nor too sophisticated) for your audience. There may be other criteria too—for example:

- Live telephone support, 8:00 P.M. to 5:00 P.M., Pacific Standard Time
- Compliance with section 508 of the Rehabilitation Act
- Discrete passwords for users
- Tracking of quiz scores

Customizing OTS Products by Adding On, Not Renovating

An alternative to buying a product outright is customizing an OTS course. Although this can mean paying the vendor to make changes to the product, it is possible that you can circumvent that expense by creating add-ons and customization of your own. The following case illustrates the idea of adding on to rather than renovating a purchased product:

Case Study: The Unlawful Workplace Harassment Problem

Our organization's policy requires mandatory training for all employees in unlawful workplace harassment. In most cases, this is delivered in a classroom-based session for new employees. But some agencies, especially those that are smaller or have employees scattered throughout the state, find meeting the mandate a hardship. Given this situation and with a realistic estimate of 250 potential users each year, we were able to make a case for using an e-learning solution.

In searching for a product, we found that harassment is a common topic for online programs: a cursory web search turned up dozens of existing courses. Many were little more than text on a screen, often with far too much in the way of technical information and legal language. Finally, we found an excellent product: EmTrain's "Preventing Unlawful Workplace Harassment" (http://www.emtrain.com). The product included pre- and postassessments, high-quality embedded video clips demonstrating realistic scenarios, good narration, professional-looking text and graphics, and some interactivity. As a bonus, the product included bookmarking (users who were interrupted could later return to the same screen without having to start the program over) and simple tracking.

Building a similar product from scratch would likely have cost $65,000; at 250 users per year, that priced out at $260 per learner—more than *ten times* the EmTrain price. But there was a problem: the EmTrain product's discussion of unlawful harassment included pregnancy and sexual orientation, which are not part of the state policy.

These were our choices:

- Build a similar program from scratch. We could not afford this in terms of time and development costs.

- Build a lower-quality program from scratch. Although this was an option, it was not a very palatable one. The topic is more effective when supported by high-quality video vignettes, and the combined issues of scattered learners and compliance with a mandate made tracking options vital.

- Purchase another program. Most we examined were of lower quality than this vendor's, and many still had the same problem of not quite fitting the state policy.

- Pay EmTrain to customize the program. The estimated cost was $20,000 in addition to the price for purchasing the OTS course. This option was out of the question given our budget constraints.

- Customize the program by adding on to rather than renovating it.

We chose the last solution. Learners accessing the program are greeted with the welcome page shown in Figure 10.1.

FIGURE 10.1. WELCOME PAGE INTRODUCING OTS COURSE

WELCOME to "Preventing Unlawful Harassment"

HOME	HELP	FAQs

The state prohibits harassment on the basis of race, age, gender, skin color, national origin, or handicapping condition.

The program you are about to view discusses pregnancy and sexual orientation as protected issues. Please be aware that the state DOES NOT recognize pregnancy and sexual orientation as protected under the Unlawful Harassment Policy; nevertheless, all employees have the right to work in an atmosphere of respect and tolerance.

As a state employee you are entitled to be treated with dignity and consideration. Should you feel you are being treated otherwise please notify your supervisor or other agency representative.

Click HERE to begin the online "Preventing Unlawful Harassment" course.

Employees accessing the program know the online course discusses exceptions to the policy, but get the message that they are still expected to exhibit tolerance and decency. EmTrain got the contract, and we have the product that meets our objectives at a price we can afford. It was truly a win-win solution and has resulted in a friendly ongoing relationship with the vendor.

Other means of adding to and customizing OTS products include pre- or postquizzes or games specific to your company; links to manuals, policies, and support tools; other online training programs (such as something simple you've built yourself to supplement the vendor information); a site with video clips specific to your work setting; and live classroom sessions.

Tips for Working with Vendors of OTS Products

Paying attention to licensing arrangements, taking advantage of trial periods and demo offers, using savvy negotiating techniques, and cultivating good relationships with vendors can result in big savings.

Basic Cost-Cutting Techniques

- Limit licenses. Vendors of off-the-shelf products often use a sliding scale of costs against number of slots: 50 slots for $200 each; 1,000 slots for $150; 5,000 slots for $100, and so on. Buy what you realistically think you will use: 5,000 slots at $100 (for a cost of $500,000) is not a deal if only 1,000 (which could have been bought for $150,000) are used.

- Share licenses. Can you partner with another unit, or even another organization, to share in the agreement? This arrangement may help you take advantage of the volume discounts often offered by vendors.

- Who ultimately pays for the course? For example, can you bill the cost back to the learner's work unit instead of paying from the training budget?

- Use demo and trial periods. Be sure the product really does work for you, your infrastructure, and your learners. Give access to as many people as you can, and get their feedback. Make sure, too, that you are asking the right people. Your new budget workshop isn't going to be used by subject matter experts like your organization's accountant. Let him or her help in evaluating it if you like, but be sure to show it to some of the first-line managers who actually will use the program.

- Work closely with the vendor to uncover any hidden issues. Some courses, for example, require a separately priced product to run them.

- Find out the vendor's schedule for product updates and whether the price you pay includes those. I once bought an e-learning product with engaging quizzes and good-quality video—by 1999 standards. Now the product looks dated and the technology primitive.

- Talk to your IT contacts. Make sure what you're buying will work with your current systems. If you have any problems later, your IT people will likely have to get involved, and fixes could be costly. Better to communicate now rather than later.

- Don't buy a vendor's product without learning firsthand about the quality of the company's help desk and technical support. A great product is worthless if nobody at the home office can figure out why a password doesn't work. I was once nearly at the point of purchase for a product when by chance I needed to call the help desk. No one there was familiar with the product I was looking at, and no one ever returned my calls. Lesson learned, fortunately just in time.

- In marketing your offerings, Vicki Cerda of Cerda Consulting reminds us (personal communication) that vendors of off-the-shelf products already have slick, tested marketing materials, from flyers to e-mail newsletters to video clips, that you can use for free.

Negotiation Strategies

- See if the vendor will agree to take care of numerical data regarding learners and product use. Can you be provided with reports and other information?

- Take advantage of the vendor's support and satellite services. Does the company provide additional products like online journals or phone mentoring? Perhaps you can negotiate to have those added at lower or no cost.

- If you are the piloting type, negotiate with the vendor to set up a pilot project that includes one or two dozen licenses for a limited period of time. This way, you are buying only what you need for the pilot, not committing to hundreds of seats ahead of time.

- Negotiate prices against future use. Suppose you know you want your e-learning enterprise to grow. That is, you expect limited use the first year but incrementally larger growth after that. Or you have a new organization and are confident about your expansion plans. An e-learning vendor may be willing to bargain now with the promise of additional business in the future. Buy what you need, but if you are confident that you'll need more later, discuss that with the vendor now.

- Remember that everything is negotiable.

Relationship with the Vendor

- Think "partnership." If you especially like a vendor's products, try to cultivate a friendly, long-term relationship with your sales rep, and as much as possible focus on quality rather than cost. Over time, a good relationship with a vendor can pay off in extra savings, enhancements, and extensions of contract periods. Cerda Consulting's Vicki Cerda advises, "Work with your vendors as strategic partners. Create a culture where the vendor also wins by doing what is best for your organization" (personal communication).

- Concentrate on quality rather than quantity of vendor relationships. Working with a few quality products is less expensive in the long run than trying to juggle dozens of different agreements.

- Give the little guys a chance. I use several small vendors and find them very easy to work with. A couple of times when I've needed something in a hurry, I've been able to get it from a small vendor very quickly (no bureaucracy: the person who answered the phone also took my order and set up my account). They also need success stories and customer endorsements, so they are usually thrilled to hear from you.

- Use the vendor's knowledge. The vendor may have great information on integration issues, for instance. Just remember that the vendor has a vested interest in your decision.

- Don't tolerate abusive or high-pressure sales tactics. A purchasing mistake, aside from being costly, is often embarrassing and public. Stick to your list of criteria, and remember the advantages of a good relationship. Is the high-pressure vendor someone you want to work with for years to come?

- The vendor relationship works both ways. I have seen indecisive colleagues ask vendors to set up pilot programs—typically a time- and energy-consuming task—for products they weren't even very serious about buying. It's not good business practice, and it's just not very fair. Don't ask to look at products until you're ready, and don't ask for proposals you don't really want.

Case Study: Sharing Licenses

Sometimes buying seats in bulk can save money if you're careful about what you really need. Once, while employed by a small state agency, I needed a product but did not have the one hundred users required to reduce the price per seat by nearly half. I contacted training friends in other small agencies and arranged a deal whereby six of us would split the one hundred slots. None of us could buy at the higher price, but all of us could afford the lower price. It was truly a win-win for the agencies and the vendor.

The Portal Alternative

So far we've looked at creating or buying perhaps one topic or course at a time. If your goal is to offer your employees a full catalogue of e-learning programs, one alternative is to contract with a vendor that provides an array of courses on many topics. For an agreed-on price, your organization buys a stated number of slots for a given period of time.

On reaching an agreement, your users would be able to access the vendor's site, such as SkillSoft's home page shown in Figure 10.2.

FIGURE 10.2. SKILLSOFT'S HOME PAGE

Used with permission of SkillSoft.

For a little more money, the vendor will set up a custom welcome page. Users will be greeted with a screen that includes your organization's own logo, colors, graphics, and other features. Figure 10.3 shows a portal site used by the state of Washington. After entering through this portal page, users can access the SkillSoft courses as well as any other e-learning programs that Washington chooses to make available.

FIGURE 10.3. WASHINGTON STATE PORTAL PAGE

Source: Used with permission of the Washington State Department of Personnel.

If you are considering buying a whole catalogue of courses, compare the catalogue to your real needs. Offering 500 courses may sound impressive, but not if 250 of them are on topics of no interest to your organization. Those in nonprofit or government agencies may have little use, for instance, for a vendor's sales training programs. Fortunately, vendors are increasingly willing to negotiate agreements that allow the client to purchase only certain topics or bundles of courses (such as all of the catalogue's computer skills or customer service programs).

Summary

Although it may seem unrealistic to those working on a shoestring, the option of buying OTS courses can be cost-efficient in the long run. Providing your managers with data about the comparable costs of creating a course yourself when an excellent OTS product already exists may help you make a case for buying even if some adding on or customizing is required. Taking advantage of cost-cutting and negotiation strategies might make the OTS choice less expensive for you. Should you decide to proceed with a purchase, be clear about your criteria, and remember the advantages of cultivating good relationships with vendors: as strategic partners, they can prove invaluable in supporting your e-learning initiative.

We have now looked at building from-scratch solutions in-house, outsourcing the building process to a contractor or developer, and purchasing ready-made products. The next chapter examines some final options about putting e-learning solutions on the web and tracking data about learners.

Part Three

Putting It All Together

11

Hosting Your Programs and Tracking Learner Data

ONCE YOU ARE READY TO LOOK at delivering e-learning to your organization's employees, you'll need to consider where the e-learning programs will reside and whether—and how—you will monitor learner participation and progress. In this chapter, we look at options for making programs available to learners, ways of tracking learner data, and managing learning systems.

Hosting

In order to deliver training online, you will need a place to put it. You may already have a company intranet or other Internet space on which your programs can reside, or you may have chosen to build your site with one of the virtual community tools, such as Yahoo Groups, which include hosting. Too, your agreements with developers and vendors of OTS products may include hosting services. But if not, you'll need to contract a service provider that will store your pages so they can be accessed by learners via the World Wide Web.

The good news is that hosting is inexpensive, especially if you aren't storing and running lots of big-file products like video clips. Most hosting providers offer packages of monthly prices ranging from $5.95 to $50.00. Packages often include hundreds of megabytes of space, e-mail autoresponders, and some space on a streaming server. This is quite a competitive field, and vendors seem to keep adding features, most recently blogs and discussion boards. Many companies offer free hosting, though there's often a catch, which may be nothing more than the appearance of an advertisement on your site's home page.

Moving files from your computer to the World Wide Web requires File Transfer Protocol (FTP) software. It's the software that connects your computer to the server hosting your product. More good news: basic FTP software can be had for **free**. Just search the web for "free FTP." Some web design products, like Dreamweaver, have FTP capability built in.

CD or Not CD?

An alternative to delivering e-learning over the web or company intranet is the CD or DVD. This can be a good option, especially for training involving video or other multimedia files that would require a great deal of bandwidth or the additional expense of a streaming server. Blank CDs can now be had for pennies apiece; blank DVDs cost more, but the price is dropping. Use of the CD or DVD format, though, prohibits the easy updating allowed by web-based programs. Change in a procedure or process, for example, might result in the need to recall existing CDs, burn new ones, and redistribute the new copies to the learners. Use of the CD or DVD format is thus a decision based on the nature of the training program and the stability of the information.

Tracking Learner Data

Once you go beyond one or two simple programs or wish to increase delivery to large numbers of learners, you'll need to find a way to keep up with all the data: who's accessing your programs, whether they're completing them, and so forth. With traditional classroom training, there's often an office assistant who handles registrations and enters completions, certifications, and test scores into an Access database or Excel spreadsheet. As you move to e-learning, you may continue having a person perform these tasks, or you may choose to find ways to do this electronically.

First Things First: What Do You Need to Do?

When determining the appropriate means of tracking data, it's important to clarify exactly what you want to track. For example, do you want to:

- Count the total number of users?
- Know who got to the last screen?
- Know who passed the test?
- Know who started *and* completed *or* didn't complete?
- Know which modules, topics, or pages were started and completed?
- Assign individual user names and passwords?
- Enable learners to register themselves?
- Mesh online with blended or all-classroom events?
- Or do you need complex capabilities such as generating dozens of different reports, statistics regarding particular test questions, and auto-billing back to the learner's work area?

These are the sorts of factors that will affect both your decision and the cost of the solution.

Some Free and Low-Cost Tracking Solutions

There are low- or no-cost ways of tracking data about your learners.

Counter. Adding a **free** JavaScript counter will tell you how many users accessed a site or a particular page on the site. Course dropout rate can also be assessed by putting different counters on the first and last pages of a program. For instance, if the hit counter on the first page reads 250 and the counter on the last page reads 230, then the assumption is that 20 people did not complete the program. It's not scientific—for example, one person may have accessed the first page twenty times—but can give you a ballpark idea about use. For those wishing to track just completions, a counter can be placed on the last screen of the course. Some hosting providers include a hit counter as part of the service agreement.

Cookies. A cookie is a snippet of information that can be "read" by the web page. Cookies can be used, for example, to track a learner's progress through modules or determine whether to allow the learner to advance through a program. Cookies in themselves are harmless, but less-than-scrupulous commercial vendors have given them a bad name. If you want to use them, talk with your IT or other computer support staff. Computers must have cookies enabled, and users may not have the skills to configure this on their own.

e-Mail. For other courses, you may just want to have proof that particular learners made it to the end. One organization offers an online "new rules for purchasing" program that is meant to provide brief information; there's no real skill building or need to test. The last screen of the course contains an e-mail link: a new e-mail window opens, already addressed to the training coordinator, and learners just click on the button to send notice of their completion. This is further managed by setting an incoming e-mail filter to send these messages to a folder labeled "new purchasing rules completion." The coordinator can then use the e-mail program to perform simple manipulations of the data, such as sorting and printing it by sender's name or date sent.

Printable Completion Form. The e-mail solution works fine if one person is the appropriate recipient for data. But some organizations may require that written documentation be kept on file or that copies of completions go to both supervisor and training coordinator. In these cases, it's easy enough to just build in a printable completion form for the employee to print, sign, and forward appropriately.

Completion Form Submit. You can create a completion form that will submit to a remote database. This can be done with a **free** survey tool like Zoomerang (http://www.zoomerang.com) or with a program set up in-house. Form submission requires technology known as *server-side scripting*; if you want the form to submit to your own server (rather than, for example, Zoomerang's), you'll need to involve your IT, computer support, or hosting service people to help you set it up, possibly at additional expense.

SCORECARD

Proof of Completion

Need: documentation that course was completed
Purchased LMS: $1,500 to $500,000
Completion form created in Word, set to submit to an e-mail account: $0

Giving a Test

If you must keep up with test scores, you have several **free** or low-cost options.

Paper and Pencil. Local learners can drop by during designated times to take a paper-and-pencil test, which you can score and record. Remote learners could be offered a test overseen by a supervisor or other proctor; some community colleges and public libraries provide assistance with proctoring tests for non-profits or government agencies.

e-Mail. A common way of testing by e-mail is arranging for a time-limited test: the instructor sends the tests to learners, who have a set amount of time in which to respond. If trust or confidentiality concerns exist, there could be a proctor or other witness to verify that the learner did take the test.

Survey Tools and Test Engines. A common use of survey tools is the creation and management of online registration and completion forms. Too, as surveys are essentially just a way of asking questions, online survey tools are widely used for administering tests. The host site will store information such as responses and date submitted and will usually allow for some manipulation of data. Many sites offer limited capability for free with more extensive functionality available at some cost. Survey maker Zoomerang's package for nonprofit organizations, which includes 10,000 survey responses and extensive customization options for the designer, is available for $350 per year. There is also a less sophisticated free version available on a time-limited basis.

More complex testing products are created by test engine providers. These offer features such as banks for storing questions and randomly generating new tests and the ability for the instructor to auto-set times for uploading and closing the test. These begin at a cost of less than $50 and increase depending on capabilities and whether the product is hosted on your server or by the vendor.

Hot Potatoes and Quia. The Hot Potatoes quiz creation product is now supported by a simple hosting and tracking service, Hot Potatoes.net (http://www.hotpota toes.net). This allows the creation of student accounts and recording of learner data. The upper-end price is $189 for 200 users or 40 courses.

The $99 ($49 for education) annual subscription to Quia games (http://www.quia.com) comes with a tracking feature that includes unlimited student accounts and access to advanced data such as statistics regarding particular questions. Figure 11.1 shows a sample of one type of score report available from Quia.

FIGURE 11.1. SAMPLE SCORE REPORT FROM QUIA

Activity: soldering 2

Overall Summary

Low Score	High Score	Mean	Median
1 (33%)	3 (100%)	2.29 (76%)	2 (67%)

Question Summary (Scroll down to student summary)

		Question	Question Type	Point Value	Number of Students Who Received Question	% of Students Who Answered Correctly	% of Students Who Answered Incorrectly
	•	1	Multiple Choice	1	7	43 %	57 %
	•	2	Multiple Choice	1	7	100 %	0 %
	•	3	Multiple Choice	1	7	86 %	14 %

Student Summary (Scroll up to question summary)

View student reports	Delete

				Student (Switch to ID)	Points (out of 3)	Score	Time Started (GMT) Time Completed (GMT)	Elapsed Time
□								
Non-enrolled students								
□	🔍		•	Betty Blue	2	67 %	2005/01/10 05:25:57 PM 2005/01/10 05:26:03 PM	00:00:06
□	🔍		•	Bill Black	1	33 %	2005/01/10 05:25:37 PM 2005/01/10 05:25:42 PM	00:00:05
□	🔍		•	Bob Brown	2	67 %	2005/01/10 05:26:36 PM 2005/01/10 05:26:41 PM	00:00:05
□	🔍		•	George Green	3	100 %	2005/01/10 05:27:06 PM 2005/01/10 05:27:12 PM	00:00:06
□	🔍		•	Opal Orange	3	100 %	2005/01/10 05:27:41 PM 2005/01/10 05:27:47 PM	00:00:06
□	🔍		•	Polly Purple	2	67 %	2005/01/10 05:28:02 PM 2005/01/10 05:28:11 PM	00:00:09
□	🔍		•	Roger Red	3	100 %	2005/01/10 05:28:26 PM 2005/01/10 05:28:37 PM	00:00:11

Key:	• No review needed	• Instructor review required	🔍 View printable report
	Grade		

Macromedia's Learning Site and Coursebuilder. Used together, the free Learning Site and Coursebuilder extensions for Dreamweaver allow the creation of learner accounts, functionality such as discrete passwords, and storage of completion information and test scores on an Access database. The database downloads with the extension and is stored in-house. The drawback may be of concern only to larger organizations: using Access limits the database to 255 users.

Moving Up: Do You Need a Learning Management System?

Do you need a learning management system (LMS)? If your organization is very small, you can likely find a fairly simple way of tracking data, such as using old-fashioned paper and pencil, providing printable completion forms, entering information into an Excel spreadsheet or Access database, or using one of the low-cost tracking services like http://www.Hot Potatoes.net. For those with 255 users or fewer, Macromedia's LearningSite, while limited in functionality, is reasonably easy to install, learn, and use, and it can serve as a workable alternative to a pricey LMS. Those using entirely in-house products, with limited tracking and reporting needs and small user bases, may find LearningSite an excellent tool.

When you're dealing with thousands of learners or juggling products from different sources, it may be time to consider a more robust LMS.

Do You Need an LMS Now?
E-learning expert Vaughan Waller advises care in deciding whether you need an LMS: "If your budget has been decimated by the LMS, then you will have no money for the learning content. It's analogous to having a superb library which has no books."

Free and Low-Cost Learning Management Systems

Several LMS tools are available under the General Public License, which means the products can be installed and used at no charge. You must use the product intact, without changes, and acknowledge the original designers and include their copyright statements. Some LMSs also are offered as open source products that allow you to modify or change the product provided you follow some guidelines specified on the company's website. All come with LMS features such as registration, tracking users, and testing. In addition to the LMS capability, different products include features like chat, discussion boards, and repositories for course documents and other files.

The best-known **free** systems are Moodle, ATutor, Angel, Interact, and Claroline. They all come highly recommended and have good track records, but the products are still free. It is not reasonable to expect 24/7 personal phone support or constant hand-holding. Too, some of the products were developed in Europe, which could present some translation issues when it comes to installation and getting help. If you want to use one of these products, work very closely with someone who understands the technology and can troubleshoot as necessary. Don't rely entirely on the designers. Many of the free LMS sites include testimonials and lists of users. Talk to these references. You may find a free product that is the right fit for you.

LMS "Lite." Some vendors now offer fairly sophisticated learning management capabilities in "lite" or "boutique" versions at greatly reduced prices, especially good news for small organizations. Try a web search for "LMS lite" and "LMS for small organizations" to see what other possibilities exist.

Alternatives: Renting an LMS, Adding On to an Existing Contract, and Using What You Have. An increasingly popular, less expensive arrangement is renting the LMS by paying a vendor to host your information on its system. You do not have to install any software or otherwise encumber your own IT people or technologies; e-learning programs are accessed through a web browser. Although these aren't free, they're less expensive than systems installed in-house. The pricing is usually arranged as a monthly fee for a set period of time. Known as the alternative service provider (ASP) model, this provides a professionally managed avenue for the company trying out an initial move into e-learning or for the small company seeking to cut costs. It's also a possible solution for any organization wanting a quick implementation. Where implementation of a complete LMS could take a year or more if done in-house, one handled with an ASP might be finished in a matter of weeks. The same cautions apply here as with buying an LMS: check references, get clear on total costs, and make sure the system fits your needs.

There is yet another possibility for those who have purchased OTS e-learning courses: large vendors of off-the-shelf courseware often provide additional LMS features at costs lower than you'd encounter if you started from scratch. See if your vendor is willing to host the rest of your e-learning program.

Finally, do you already have a system in place that might do this for you? If your HR office uses PeopleSoft or Oracle, for instance, you may already have access to much of the functionality that you need.

If You Decide to Purchase an LMS

The information here is meant only to round out this chapter's general discussion of tracking learner data. The purchase of a robust LMS can easily move into the six-figure range and is thus beyond the realm of a shoestring solution. Here, though, are some basic considerations for those interested in the cost-saving aspects of choosing an LMS.

Benefits versus Features. In evaluating an LMS, it's important to differentiate benefits from features. Benefits add value; features tend to add price. An analogy is that of buying a new car: benefits are the must-haves, such as an engine and wheels. Features are add-ons like heated seats and power windows. Table 11.1 illustrates the difference between typical must-have versus nice-to-have LMS functionalities.

TABLE 11.1. COMPARISON OF MUST-HAVE BENEFITS VERSUS NICE-TO-HAVE LMS FEATURES

Benefit	Feature
Integrates with HR systems	Multilanguage capability
Works with most authoring tools	Includes hundreds of color templates
Tracks learner completion	Creates personalized "welcome" page for each learner
Intuitive and easy to learn	Bulletin boards
Handles registration	PowerPoint conversion
Provides necessary reports	Chat rooms
Tracks test scores	Streaming media capability
Handles billing	Tracks costs for return-on-investment measurements for individual managers' budgets

The purchase of even a low-cost LMS will likely require that you sell the need to management and budget officers. Clarifying the difference between benefit and feature can be crucial in this discussion. A training manager friend, a very techno-savvy type, loves bells and whistles. He found a good LMS at a good price, with some features that added only marginally to the cost. But in presenting his request to purchase it, he kept emphasizing features that sounded like expensive add-ons to his audience. Their response: "We don't need all that. Go find us something cheaper." Essentially they wanted a Honda but felt he was trying to justify buying a Cadillac. Be able to articulate, for yourself and others, how the LMS will benefit your organization.

If you've decided to start shopping for an LMS, consider the following strategies for reducing costs.

Basic Tips for Cutting Costs

- Use demo and trial periods. As Bose's Michael McGinnis says, this gives you a chance to "kick the tires" before you buy.

- How many licenses do you really need? Make a realistic estimate of your number of users. You can always add more later.

- Talk to references. The three most recent will likely be able to tell you how the company is functioning now. If possible, talk with other people in the company too, including the vendor's technical staff.

- Establish your criteria before talking with vendors. Knowing what you need will help keep you from being talked into something you don't.

Negotiation Strategies

- When looking at benefits and features, consider the idea of adding on: buy what you must have now, and add on what you'd like to have later. Make sure, though, that the cost of those add-ons is within reason.

- Does pricing include:

  Training for your staff in using the LMS?

  Help and tech support, especially the first year?

International users?

Addition of new users in the future?

Upgrades and updates? For how long?

- Does the contract include:

Provisions should the vendor go out of business or be acquired by another company? (Warning: This is common.)

An "out" (nonperformance) clause if the system does not perform as promised?

An out clause or change in pricing should deadlines for implementation fail to be met?

What's the Real Cost of the LMS? Often the presenting price of an LMS is just the tip of the iceberg: industry figures put the cost of LMS implementation and other expenses at 50 to 100 percent above the purchase price. When shopping for an LMS, find out what other costs you may be facing:

- Time and costs associated with learning about the vendors
- Licenses
- Delivery
- Expenses associated with any pilot projects
- Consulting fees for implementation
- Consulting fees during integration
- Training staff to use the LMS
- Expenses associated with change management
- Annual maintenance fees
- Service fees
- Fees for technical support and other help
- Number of staff needed to operate and maintain the product
- Upgrades
- Scalability and cost of adding more users

An LMS may well be the most expensive single purchase you will ever make (if, in fact, you need to make it at all). While full-blown learning management systems may be described as expensive, they are not necessarily overpriced. These are remarkably complex, sophisticated products that can, if they fit your needs, provide enormous savings in terms of data entry and retrieval expenses. Saving money on an LMS may be less a matter of finding an inexpensive product and more a matter of not making expensive mistakes. The best course of action is to get educated. Read articles, attend workshops, and sit in on vendor demonstrations. Keep asking questions until you get answers you understand. As the field continues to evolve, search the web for "LMS Checklist" and "Choosing an LMS" to be sure you're working with up-to-date information. And if you are seriously considering purchasing an LMS costing tens of thousands of dollars or more, an excellent investment is hiring a consultant with the expertise you need to help you make a good choice of product and create the contract that works best for you.

Learning Content Management System

LCMSs help you organize and use your objects. This is very advanced technology and, as with the LMS, you may be looking at the mid–six figures. If you're a small shop, you can likely manage this on your own by taking care in building libraries of content and objects you create. If you are planning to build an extensive, long-term e-learning initiative involving dozens of courses, you may need to look at an LCMS. There is no really cheap or open-source product for this yet. That's probably coming, though, so keep your ear to the ground for it, and check my website, http://www.bozarthzone.com, to see if there are new developments.

Tracking: A Recap

As you've seen in this chapter, managing learning can range from the simple paper-and-pencil test to an elaborate and expensive LMS. Think carefully about your real needs. Table 11.2 will help you match your needs and problems with a workable solution.

TABLE 11.2. FINDING SOLUTIONS TO PROBLEMS

Problem	Solution
To know how many accessed	Free hit counter
To know who accessed	Free survey ("registration form")
To know who reached last page	Printable completion form
	Free survey on last page ("completion form")
	E-mail completion
To know that Bill Smith scored 90 percent on a test	Give Bill a paper-and-pencil test
	E-mail Bill the test with a time limit for taking it; have him e-mail it back to you for scoring
	Use Quia quiz
	Use Macromedia Coursebuilder Learning Site
Compiling data	Free survey tool
	Access database
Managing products from a number of sources	LMS
Tracking blended learning	Robust LMS will also support, for example, classroom scheduling and instructors
Link training reporting systems to HR reporting systems	LMS or custom-built solution

Summary

Although choosing a hosting solution should not prove especially difficult or costly, the LMS decision is likely one of the most complex and expensive you'll ever make. First, ask yourself whether you really need one: Do you have lots of products, lots of learners, or the need to prove completion of training for legally problematic certifications and licensure? Is your scope so large that paper-and-pencil testing and e-mail-and-Access registration are no longer viable? Do the free LMSs fail somehow to meet your needs? If so, then you may be ready to look at buying (or renting) a commercial LMS solution.

Once you start looking at the options, you'll have a dazzling array of choices. Take your time, be very clear on what you really need, and buy the solution that solves your problems.

We have now explored the many options available to the organization seeking to develop or purchase inexpensive e-learning programs. Let's move on now to the final chapter, where we'll look at ways organizations have combined these options to create complete solutions on a shoestring.

Application

N OW LET'S PUT IT all together. In this chapter, we'll first take a closer look at applying our decision-making process to some real problems. Then we'll examine ways of assembling assorted tools to create complete programs at little or no cost. We've seen many tools and techniques in the past chapters; in approaching an e-learning project, think of them as building blocks, each one adding to and interlocking with the others.

Mixing It Up: Matching Approaches to Learners and Learning Styles

Just as with classroom training, it's vital to choose strategies that will support and engage learners who have varying preferences and learning styles. Although different ideas come in and out of vogue, some of the better-known sources of information on learning styles include David Kolb's concept of the learning cycle (1984) and Howard Gardner's ideas on multiple intelligences

(1993). While there are many theories, most incorporate the notions that learners tend to think in different ways (for instance, some of us think in a linear, sequential fashion, while others favor random exploration of ideas) and have preferences in the way they wish to have information presented to them (for example, some of us prefer to read new information, while others want to hear the information presented). Preferences and styles can shift, of course, depending on the learning task and the learner's level of proficiency with a new skill. In creating online learning, particularly of the self-directed variety, it's vital that the designer work to engage, stimulate, and provide information in ways that accommodate differing preferences and styles. Figure 12.1, adapted from the Herrmann (1989) model of brain dominance, is meant as one way

FIGURE 12.1. MATCHING E-LEARNING APPROACHES TO LEARNER STYLES

Source: Copyright The Ned Herrmann Group, 2004.

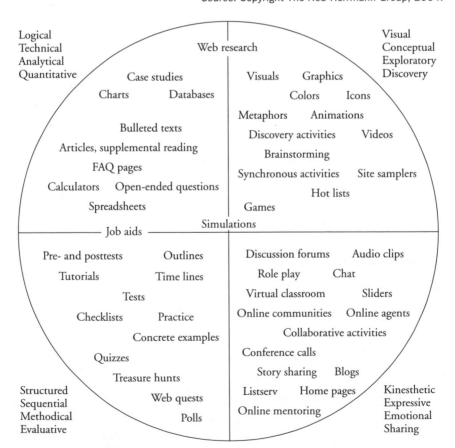

of situating the material in this book against the notion of learning styles. Whichever particular theory of learning you subscribe to, think of the figure as a means of sorting out tools and approaches into general categories for different types of learners. Items inside each quadrant are those especially appropriate to the preferences and styles listed in the areas outside each quadrant.

Cases: The Buy-or-Build Decision

The situations described below present the decision-making issues that resulted in three common e-learning solutions: building in-house, adding on to an OTS product, and outsourcing development of a custom product.

Situation 1: e-Mail Etiquette

Situation. Due to legal considerations, management requested training on e-mail etiquette for all staff. The program required some propriety information and reference to the nature of the company's work. It would be deployed to 1,300 employees and had to be delivered very quickly.

Solution. Build.

Product. The product was a narrated, animated PowerPoint presentation for delivery across multiple formats. The completed program was converted from a large PowerPoint file to a much smaller Flash movie file through use of a converter product, available for free for a ten-day trial period or for a purchase price of $399.

SCORECARD

e-Mail Etiquette

Actual cost of in-house development: $500 (designer's salary)
Cost comparison:
  Cost of more sophisticated program; for instance, program using video developed in-house: $25,000
  Cost of hiring outside firm to develop: $45,000
  Cost of similar off-the-shelf product for 2,000 users: $50,000

Situation 2: The Hiring Process

Situation. On investigating a rash of problems with new employees, it was discovered that many of the company's newer managers, most working in remote sites on different shifts, were very weak on interviewing skills and specifics of the company's hiring process. The training unit was given a budget of $3,000 to develop a training solution.

It was found that only a small part of the information was company specific (such as the details of the organization's paperwork path from resignation of the former employee to hiring of the replacement employee). In addition, some content deemed important to the project (videos of effective and ineffective interviews) would be difficult and expensive to create from scratch. The number of projected users for three years was estimated at 100.

Solution. Purchase and customize an off-the shelf product.

Product. The training unit found a vendor with an online interviewing course that included extensive information on writing position descriptions and excellent examples of well-conducted and poorly handled job interviews. Although the product was fine, the position description content was not relevant to the organization's needs. The training unit negotiated with the vendor to purchase only the modules on interviewing skills. In-house training staff developed supplemental online materials, including pre- and postassessments built with Coursebuilder, an online bank of good interview questions, an animated chart illustrating the company's paperwork flow, and a site with hiring-related support tools such as a quick-check preinterview form and a reminder about the rules of reference checking. The purchased product on interviewing skills is sandwiched between appropriate pieces of the company-specific information.

Situation 3: New Employee Orientation

Situation. The orientation workshop for new state government employees is an information program designed to educate new employees about health insurance options, deferred savings plans, retirement benefits, vacation and sick leave policies, tuition reimbursement, and other benefits. The program also includes paperwork required of new employees such as tax forms and cre-

SCORECARD

Hiring

Cost for 100 slots for only the interviewing portion of the vendor's program:
$2,000
Quizzes with scaffolded feedback created in Coursebuilder: $0
Registration form created with Zoomerang: $0
Concluding subject sampler: $0

dential verification waivers. In the past, the program was offered as live classroom training by most agencies; there was no uniformity, little consistency in messaging, and rampant redundancy and duplication of effort. For instance, in a half-mile square within the downtown state government complex, no fewer than eight different agencies offered this program as a classroom course. Thus, in the span of one month, eight different trainers used eight different classrooms to train as few as one or two people at a time on the same material.

An e-learning approach would solve many of these problems as well as ensure that new employees would get the information in a timely manner. The program did involve organization-specific language and forms and would reach out to far more than 500 users.

Solution. Build an online program. An additional cost-saving solution was to outsource development to graduate students.

Product. A team of North Carolina State University graduate students enrolled in an advanced instructional design course agreed to develop an online new employee orientation program for state employees for their semester project. The proposed program would allow new employees to complete such items as tax, retirement system, and health insurance enrollment forms and present basic information about employment and benefits. The project team delivered a package complete with lesson plans, storyboards, sample templates, and other materials, such that a programmer or web designer could take the materials and create a working online course. The team included a student with web design experience who could provide preliminary sample programming. On completion of the course design, a programmer was contracted to develop the final working product and remains on contract on a per-hour basis to perform any updates. There is a final plus: because the completed program cost so little to create, it is provided for free to all agencies and employees wishing to use it.

SCORECARD

New Employee Orientation

Design and development carried out by a team of graduate students as a project for an advanced instructional design class: $0

Programming and web development performed by part-time contractor: $1,500

Total cost for complete online orientation program: $1,500

Cost comparison:

Cost for comparable program with less customization using a vendor (average estimate): $14,500

Cost for development by a full-time training development team: $35,000

In choosing solutions, it is crucial to think through issues such as a realistic estimate of numbers of learners, needs versus wants, and the reality of the available budget.

Cases: Assembling Tools and Approaches to Create e-Learning Programs

This section describes cases outlining the ways different tools and approaches can be configured to create complete, quality e-learning solutions on a shoestring.

Blended Program: Safety Procedures

The blended program includes classroom practice in first aid, emergency evacuation procedures, and safe lifting techniques. Following training, the participant e-mail addresses are added to a group list; trainees then receive a short "safety tips" e-mail each month. Additional reminders take the form of three-minute animated PowerPoint shows placed on the company intranet. There are free hit counters on the home pages of these reminders to help assess use. Cost: $0.

Purchased OTS Leadership Program

This small organization has a few midlevel managers scattered around the Southeast. To obtain basic leadership skills training, the organization negotiated a contract with a purchase price of $99 per learner, with no requirement for a minimum number of slots, and billing after, rather than prior to, use. The vendor provides tracking and reports. The cost of the leadership course is billed back to the learner's work unit so does not come from training funds. Cost: $99 to the learner's unit; $0 to the training department.

Free Program from the Web

A fourteen-member nonprofit agency needed to show a good-faith effort in providing sexual harassment training. The training coordinator performed a web search for "sexual harassment online training" that turned up nine good free programs, one of them exceptionally well done. A link to this site was sent to all staff, and screen shots of the program were printed out and kept on file as proof of content covered. Employees were also sent a copy of the agency policy (via e-mail, with a "read receipt" tag to confirm that employees had in fact received the material) along with a site sampler with links to harassment law, famous cases, pitfalls, and an interactive "is it or isn't it harassment" quiz. Cost: $0.

Custom Computer Skills Program

A business with 150 employees needed all staff trained in a new industry-specific computer application. Because there was no off-the-shelf training product, this required the development of custom content. Instructional design was done by in-house training staff who created storyboards and then hired and oversaw a high school senior as a summer intern (at a total cost of $750). The student, provided with a good machine and DemoCharge software for capturing animated screen shots (http://www.yessoftware.com, $49.95), created the tutorials and embedded them into web pages created with Dreamweaver. The organization added on the free Coursebuilder and Learning Site extensions for Dreamweaver in order to send test scores and track completion via an MS Access database. Cost: $799.95, or $5.33 per learner.

Extended Online Trainer Skills Course

This course consists of six lessons with one lesson provided each week. It is offered through a free online community (similar to Yahoo Groups and MSN Groups), requires no development of web pages, and there is no fee for hosting. The password-protected site consists of:

- A home page, changed each week to welcome students to the new lesson

- Weekly reading assignments uploaded to the site's "Files" section as Word and PDF documents, a brief PowerPoint show narrated by the instructor offering some additional information about the week's topic, and instructions for accessing other lesson materials

- Weekly discussion assignments completed over the site's message board

- Weekly chat assignments completed over the site's chat feature

- In the site's "members" area, links to student home pages

- A weekly test created with the "Polls" tool; grades, provided using confidential student codes, are recorded in the "Database" section

- A calendar function that sends auto-reminders about assignment due dates

Figures 12.2 and 12.3 show the home page and a sample course page. Cost: $0

Sales Training: Overcoming Customer Objections

Because the organization's salespeople work by e-mail and telephone, it made more sense to offer the program online rather than live (it takes different skills

FIGURE 12.2. HOME PAGE OF ONLINE COURSE HOSTED BY FREE ONLINE COMMUNITY

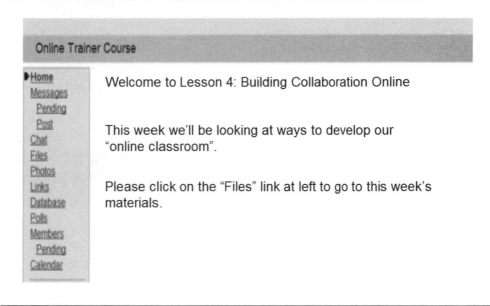

FIGURE 12.3. ASSIGNMENTS CREATED FROM FREE SITE'S "FILES" PAGE

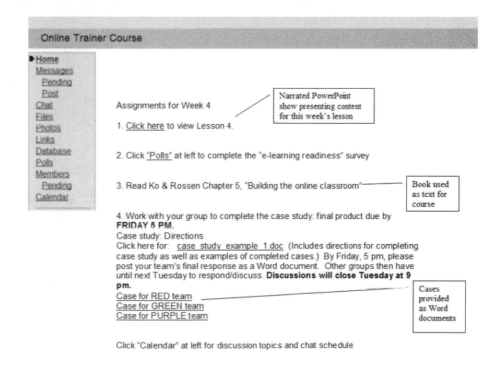

to interact with someone by e-mail—absent verbal and visual cues—than it does to talk face-to-face with a client). The solution included:

- Video vignettes created with repurposed video from the company's training library

- Content created in Dreamweaver

- A printable "critical skills" card listing steps to follow

- Online conference calls to provide skill practice

- Follow-up support with monthly video chat sessions, via Yahoo Messenger, during which learners can share their experiences and tips

Six Stress Tips for Patient Care Professionals

The small community hospital wanted to offer some help and send the message that it was sensitive to the situation of its own workers. Rather than use a purchased product, the training department quickly developed a stand-alone eight-minute narrated PowerPoint show, converted to Flash, that included still photos of some of the hospital staff and the hospital itself. The PowerPoint show linked to a "relaxation" game created with Quia ($99 per year for noneducation organizations). The program concluded with a subject sampler listing myriad stress management, exercise, and relaxation sites.

Summary

Remember as you seek to develop e-learning solutions on a shoestring that you have many resources, lots of them **free**, including design tools and graphics, game and quiz builders, and tracking and management tools. Be creative: learn to mix and match to create the programs that suit your needs. While I certainly wish you all the money you want, I also hope you find that the things you build, or creatively buy, prove to be better than the expensive options others may own. Working on a shoestring, at least for awhile, will help you make better decisions in the future.

At the beginning of this book, I promised to convince you that e-learning doesn't have to cost a bundle, and I hope I've succeeded in showing you that having no money is a challenge rather than an obstacle. I hope you feel encouraged that good e-learning solutions are within your grasp and that you are empowered to act on your new knowledge. Please contact me via my website, http://www.bozarthzone.com, and tell me how working on a shoestring is going. I plan to add a showcase of products that readers create and send me. You can accomplish a great deal with creativity, tenacity, resourcefulness, and the willingness to try. Keep trying, keep learning, and share what you know.

References and Other Sources

Bernath, U., & Hulsmann, T. (2004, March 4–6). Low cost/high outcomes approaches in open, distance and e-learning. In U. Bernath & A. Szucs (Eds.), *Supporting the learner in distance education and e-learning* (pp. 485–491). Proceedings of the third EDEN research workshop. Oldenburg, Germany: Carl von Ossietzky University.

Bersin, J. (2004). Is PowerPoint an e-learning tool? Is rapid e-learning here at last? Retrieved January 13, 2005, from http://www.bersin.com/tips_techniques/Breeze.asp.

Beuerlein, E. The skinny on job aids. Retrieved January 13, 2005, from http://coe.sdsu.edu/eet/Articles/jobaids2/index.htm.

Blaufuss Medical Multimedia Laboratories. Heart sounds tutorial. Retrieved January 13, 2005, from http://www.blaufuss.org/tutorial.

Clark, D. (2002). Wholesome Path case study. Retrieved January 12, 2005, from http://www.nwlink.com/_donclark/hrd.

Clark, R., & Mayer. M. (2003). *E-learning and the science of instruction.* San Francisco: Pfeiffer.

Corrigan, A., & Drinis, E. (2002). The art of the quick reference. Retrieved January 13, 2005, from http://www.e-learningguru.com/articles/art_misc_2.htm.

Dobbs, K. (2000). Simple moments of learning. *Training 35*(1), 52–58.

Francis, L. (2002, January). Buy versus build: A battle of needs. *Learning Circuits.* Article retrieved January 13, 2005, from http://www.learningcircuits.org/2002/jan2002/elearn.html; flow chart image retrieved January 12, 2005, from http://www.learningcircuits.org/NR/rdonlyres/E972640D-A1F3–4A41–802F-BE8D830825E1/0/buy_build.pdf.

Gardner, H. (1993). *Frames of mind: The theory of multiple intelligences.* (Rev. ed.) New York: Basic Books.

Gaylord, T., & Tolliver, D. (2003, August). Sharing e-learning services: Former rivals improve education while stretching dollars. Retrieved January 7, 2005, from http://www.thejournal.com/magazine.vault/A4476.cfm.

Hequet, M. (2003, September). The state of the e-learning market. *Training,* pp. 24–29.

Herrmann, N. (1989). *The creative brain.* Lake Lure, NC: Ned Herrmann Group.

Hess, G., & Hancock, S. (2001). *Using Dreamweaver to create e-learning.* Vancouver, WA: Rapidintake Press.

Hofmann, J. (2003). *The synchronous trainer's survival guide.* San Francisco: Pfeiffer.

Hofmann, J. (2004). *Live and online! Tips, techniques, and ready-to-use activities for the virtual classroom.* San Francisco: Pfeiffer.

Keil, K., & Kruse, K. (2000). *Technology-based training.* San Francisco: Pfeiffer.

Kolb, D. (1984). *Experiential learning: Experience as the source of learning and development.* Upper Saddle River, NJ: Prentice Hall.

Lopuck, L. *Web design for dummies.* Hoboken, NJ: Wiley, 2001.

McGinnis, M. Buying an LMS on a shoestring budget. Retrieved January 10, 2004, from http://www.teamxtend.com/shoestring.htm.

Millar, G. (2004). Learning objects 101: A primer for neophytes. Retrieved January 13, 2005, from http://online.bcit.ca/sidebars/02november/inside-out-1.htm.

Perry, T. (2002). E-learning or classroom decision criteria checklist. Retrieved January 13, 2005, from http://coastal.com.

Reiser, R. (2001). A history of instructional design and technology, part II: A history of instructional design. *Educational Technology Research & Development* 49(2), 57–67.

Rogers, E. *Diffusion of innovations.* (4th ed.). New York: Free Press, 1995.

Shank, P., & Sitze, A. (2004). *Making sense of online learning.* San Francisco: Pfeiffer.

Shepherd, C. Content builders: Tools for e-learning authors. Retrieved May 1, 2005, from http://www.fastrak-consulting.co.uk/tactix/features/content.htm.

Smith, B. E., & Bebank, A. (2004). *Creating web pages for dummies.* Hoboken, NJ: Wiley.

Thiagarajan, S. (2004). Zero-cost e-Learning: Email games. Retrieved January 12, 2005, from http://www.thiagi.com/email.html.

Toth, T. (2003). *Technology for trainers.* Alexandria, VA: ASTD.

Wager, W., & McKay, J. (2002). EPSS: Visions and viewpoints. In R. A. Reiser & J. V. Dempsey (Eds.), *Trends and issues in instructional design and technology.* Upper Saddle River, NJ: Merrill/Prentice Hall.

Additional Resources

LISTED HERE, BY CHAPTER, are resources mentioned throughout the book (including some already listed in "References and Other Sources") along with additional suggestions for research and review. Also check http://www. bozarthzone.com for updates, revisions, and new additions.

Introduction

- Search Engines

  Google http://www.google.com

  Alta Vista http://www.altavista.com

  MSN http://www.msn.com

  Lycos http://www.lycos.com

Chapter One: e-Learning: Some Basics

- e-Learning Centre http://www.e-learningcentre.co.uk

- Shank, P., & Sitze, A. (2004). *Making sense of online learning.* San Francisco: Pfeiffer.

Chapter Three: Building Simple Pages and Programs

- Learning Web Design

  Lopuck, L. (2001). *Web design for dummies.* Hoboken, NJ: Wiley.

  Microsoft http://office.microsoft.com

  Smith, B. E., & Bebank, A. (2004). *Creating web pages for dummies.* Hoboken, NJ: Wiley.

  Toth, T. (2003). *Technology for trainers.* Alexandria, VA: ASTD.

- Support for Microsoft Products

  Microsoft http://office.microsoft.com

  Microsoft's education site http://www.microsoft.com/Education/Default.aspx

- Accessibility

  Section 508 http://www.section 508.gov

- HTML, Web Development, and Authoring Tools

  Notepad http://www.notepad.org

  Dreamweaver, Coursebuilder, and Learning Site http://www.macromedia.com

  Authorware http://www.macromedia.com

  ReadyGo! http://www.readygo.com

  Toolbook http://sumtotalsystems.com

  Dazzlermax http://www.dazzler.net

- Free Communities

  Yahoo Groups http://www.yahoo.com

  MSN Groups http://www.msn.com

- Quia Class Pages http://www.quia.com

Chapter Four: Enhancing Basic Programs

- Art

  Animation Factory http://www.animfactory.com

  The Free Site http://www.thefreesite.com

- Templates

  Elated http://www.elated.com

- Online Agents

  MS Agent http://www.microsoft.com/msagent

  Using MS Agent with PowerPoint http://www.voxproxy.com

- Windows MovieMaker http://www.microsoft.com/windowsxp/ using/moviemaker/default.mspx

- Coursebuilder (add-on to Dreamweaver) http://www. macromedia.com

- Crazytalk ("cartoonizing" software) http://reallusion.com

- Microsoft Windows Producer http://www.microsoft.com/windows/ windowsmedia/technologies/producer.aspx

Chapter Five: Creating Inexpensive Quizzes, Games, Searches, Puzzles, and Simulations

- Training specialist William Horton http://www.horton.com

- e-Mail Games

  The Thiagi Group http://www.thiagi.com

- Quiz Tools

  Hot Potatoes from Half-Baked Software http://web.uvic.ca/ hrd/halfbaked

  Coursebuilder (add-on to Dreamweaver) http://www. macromedia.com

- Learning Coursebuilder

Hess, G., & Hancock, S. (2001). *Using Dreamweaver to create e-learning.* Vancouver, WA: Rapidintake Press.

- Flash and Java Games

  Collaborative Learning Systems http://www.collaborativelearningsystems.com

  Quia http://www.quia.com

  Free Flash player http://www.macromedia.com

  Web quests http://www.webquest.sdsu.edu

  Simulations: Forio http://forio.com

Chapter Six: Creating Low-Cost Collaboration

- Yahoo Groups http://www.yahoo.com

- MSN Groups http://www.msn.com

- Hofmann, J. (2003). *The synchronous trainer's survival guide.* San Francisco: Pfeiffer.

- Hofmann, J. (2004). *Live and online! Tips, techniques, and ready-to-use activities for the virtual classroom.* San Francisco: Pfeiffer.

- Watkins, R. (2005). *75 e-learning activities: making online learning interactive.* San Francisco: Pfeiffer.

- Free blog http://www.blog.com

- Free discussion boards http://www.voy.com

- Free e-mail

  Yahoo (yahoo mail) http://www.yahoo.com

  MSN (hotmail) http://www.msn.com

- Free Surveys

  Zoomerang: http://www.zoomerang.com

  Freeonlinesurveys http://www.freeonlinesurveys.com

- Wiki http://www.Wikipedia.com

- Don Clark's human resource development page http://www.nwlink.com/~donclark/hrd.html

Chapter Seven: Creating Performance Support Tools on a Shoestring

- Kevin Kruse, e-learning guru http://www.e-learningguru.com
- San Diego State University's *Encyclopedia of Educational Technology* http://coe.sdsu.edu/eet/

Chapter Eight: Leveraging Resources

- Professional Organizations

  American Society for Training and Development
  http://www.astd.org

  International Society for Performance Improvement
  http://www.ispi.org

  National Association for Government Training and
  Development http://www.nagtad.org

  Web-based: e-Learning Guild http://www.elearningguild.com

- Flash/web designer Jim Gray http://www.jfgray.org
- SCORM guidelines http://www.adlnet.org
- *SideBars,* an online publication of the British Columbia Institute of Technology http://online.bcit.ca/sidebars
- Student Projects

  Texas State University http://www.english.txstate.edu/
  student_projects.htm

  Agatha Taormina's "Writing for the Web" course site http://www.
  nvcc.edu/home/ataormina/eng123/stshowcase.htm

Chapter Nine: Paying Someone Else to Build for You

- Kevin Kruse, e-learning guru http://www.e-learningguru.com

Chapter Ten: Buying Off-the-Shelf Courses

- EmTrain's "Preventing Unlawful Workplace Harassment"
  http://www.emtrain.com

Chapter Eleven: Hosting Your Programs and Tracking Learner Data

- Zoomerang http://www.zoomerang.com

- Surveymonkey http://www.surveymonkey.com

- Hot Potatoes hosting service http://www.hotpotatoes.net

- Quia http://www.quia.com

- McGinnis, M. Buying an LMS on a shoestring budget. Retrieved January 10, 2004, from http://www.teamxtend.com/ shoestring.htm.

Chapter Twelve: Application

- Animated screen shot capture http://www.yessoftware.com

Additional Suggested Resources

- Ruth Colvin Clark has written extensively on e-learning and is especially good on the use of visuals (http://www.clarktraining.com).

- University of New Brunswick professor Elizabeth Burge offers academic-based thoughtful comments on distance learning (http://www.unbf.ca/education/welcome/people/burge.html).

- Filamentality (http://www.filamentality.com/wired/fil/). This **free** site/tool is like a virtual coach, guiding you through picking a topic, searching the web, gathering sites and links, and helping you spin your ideas into online training activities. Think of Filamentality as an organizing tool. Filamentality also will store your files for **free** for at least a year. Even if you do not use the Filamentality service, the site is rich with ideas for building activities.

- McGinnis, M. E. (2002, October). Learning on a Shoestring. *Learning and Training Innovations.* Retrieved January 17, 2005, from http:// www.elearningmag.com/ltimagazinearticle/articleDetail.jsp?id=35287. McGinnis tells the story of his organization's move to e-learning using a homemade library of repurposed PowerPoint shows and surplused computers housed in the company cafeteria.

- Wenger, E., McDermott, R., & Snyder, W. (2002). *Cultivating communities of practice.* Boston: Harvard Business School Press. Solid advice for creating and developing a community of practice.

Index

A

Access, Microsoft, 49

Accessibility, 46

Action buttons, PowerPoint, 34

Action mazes, 96

Activities, collaborative: case studies, 110–111; e-tutoring, 112–113; icebreakers, 106–107; online conversations, 105–106; role plays, 111–112, 113; storytelling, 113; team assignments, 108–110

Agents: defined, 59; using, 59–61

American Society for Training and Development, 128

Americans with Disabilities Act, 33

Animated talking characters, 59–61

Animations, PowerPoint, 35–37

Apple's QuickTime player, 25, 62

Applets, defined, 83

Ashcombe School, England's, 126

Assessment, technology, 24–27

Assignments, team, 108–110

Asynchronous collaboration: defined, 99; synchronous versus, 99–101; tools, 103–105

Audience for this book, 2–3

Audio files, 62–63

Audioconferencing, 102

Authoring products, 52

B

Bartering, 129

Basic e-learning programs: building, 31–54; enhancing, 55–69

Bebank, A., 32

Bernath, U., 127

Bid review process, 143–144

Binoculars icon, purpose of, 6

Blended programs, 13, 182–183

Blogs: defined, 104; wikis versus, 105

Books, recommended: *Creating Web Pages for Dummies*, 32; *Live and Online!*, 103; *Making Sense of Online Learning*, 137; *Synchronous Trainer's Survival*

Guide, 103; *Technology for Trainers,* 32; *Using Dreamweaver to Create e-Learning,* 72; *Web Design for Dummies,* 32

Brown, S., 122

Building e-learning programs: advanced design tools for, 49–54; books on, 32; enhancements, 55–69; inventory checklist for, 21–24; leveraging resources and, 125–133; MS Office Products for, 32–49; user considerations in, 24–27; wants versus needs, 27–30. *See also* Outsourced projects

Buy-versus-build decision: flowchart of, 16–17; off-the-shelf courses and, 150; situations illustrating, 179–182

C

Calculators, as job aids, 120, 121

Case study activity, 110–111

CD or DVD format, 164

Cerda, V., 154, 155

Chapter summaries, 3–4

Characters, talking, 59–61

Chat, 101

Checklist, Inventory, 21–23

Checklists, as job aids, 116, 120

Clark, D., 110

Clark, R., 59

Classroom activities: costs of, 10; e-learning combined with, 13, 182–183; examples of, 11–12

Classrooms, virtual, 102–103

Clip art: editing, 46–48; free, 55–56

Collaboration, asynchronous: defined, 99; synchronous versus, 99–101; tools, 103–105

Collaboration, synchronous: asynchronous versus, 99–101; defined, 99; tools, 101–103

Collaborative activities: case studies, 110–111; e-tutoring, 112–113; icebreakers, 106–107; online conversations, 105–106; role plays, 111–112, 113; storytelling, 113; team assignments, 108–110

Collaborative Learning Systems, 82, 83

Completion forms, 166–167, 169, 175

Computer skills, required, 4–5

Computers: access to, 24, 26; top-of-the-line, 23–24; Windows environment, 4, 23

Conference calling, 102

Conversations, online, 105–106

Cookies: defined, 166; as security issue, 25

Copyright and sharing, 125–127

Corrigan, A., 118

Cost estimates of e-learning, 1–2

Cost issues, outsourcing: bid review process, 143–144; contracts, 138, 145–146; cost factors, 139–141; cost-cutting strategies, 141–142, 144; hidden costs, 142–143; pricing, 138–139

Costly mistakes, 14–15

Counters, hit, 165–166, 175, 183

Coursebuilder, Macromedia: description of, 63–64; puzzles built with, 95; as quiz tool, 72

Creating Web Pages for Dummies, 32

Crossword puzzles, 94

Custom development: complexity of, 137–138; contracts for, 138, 145–146; cost factors, 139–141; cost-cutting strategies for, 141–142, 144; hidden costs of, 142–143; pricing, 138–139; request for proposal, 143–144; summary on, 147; vendor criteria, 145–146

Customizing off-the-shelf products, 16, 151–153, 180

D

Decision tables, 120

Design templates, free, 56–58

Design tips: hot lists, 66, 67–68; hot spots, 68, 69; site samplers, 66–67; themes and metaphors, 65–66

Discussion boards, 104

Dobbs, K., 115

Downloads, free Microsoft, 59–62

Drag-and-drop quiz, 73, 78, 79

Dreamweaver program: Coursebuilder and, 63–64, 72; description of, 50; FTP capability, 164; as standard program, 143

Dreamweaver to Create e-Learning, Using, 72

Drinis, E., 118

Dropout rate, tracking, 165, 175

DVD or CD format, 164

Dynamic HTML (DHTML), defined, 65

E

Early adopters, 15

e-Coach, defined, 113

Elated.com, 56–58

e-Learning: advantages of, 10, 18; buying versus building, 16–17, 150, 179–182; decision to use, 10–12; defined, 9–10; examples of, 182–186; wants versus needs in, 27–29

e-Learning programs: building basic, 31–54; enhancing, 55–69; hosting services for, 163–164; off-the-shelf courses, 149–159; outsourcing development of, 137–147

e-Learning Solutions on a Shoestring: audience for, 2–3, 4–5; binoculars icon in, 6; chapter summaries, 3–4; companion website for, 4, 187; disclaimer, 6–7; scorecard boxes in, 5

Electronic performance support system (EPSS), 117

e-Mail: as asynchronous tool, 105; as e-learning tool, 51–52; games, 80–81; testing by, 167; tracking data with, 166

e-Mail etiquette case study, 179

e-Mentor, defined, 113

e-Tutor, defined, 113

Excel, Microsoft: description of, 49; games created with, 89

F

File size and multimedia, 63

File Transfer Protocol (FTP) software, 164

Fill-in-the-blank quizzes, 73, 76–78

Find command, MS Word, 118, 119

Firewall issues, 25, 27, 101

Fixed-bid price, defined, 139

Flash and Java game templates, 82–85

Flash player: PowerPoint files and, 39–40; in technology assessment, 25, 27 Flash video clips, 62, 133

Flowchart, buy-versus-build decision, 16–17

Flowcharts, as job aids, 116, 120

Forio's Broadcast Express software, 96

Form tools, Microsoft Word, 44, 45

Forms, completion, 166–167, 169, 175

"Four Heads" game, 81

Free clip art, 55–56

Free design templates, 56–58

Free downloads: Microsoft Agent, 59–61; Microsoft Producer, 62; Windows MovieMaker, 61–62, 133

Free tools and options: finding, 5–6; off-the-shelf solutions, 16–17

Freeware, defined, 58

FrontPage, Microsoft, 50–51

G

Games: e-mail, 80–81; reasons for using, 80; tools for creating, 80–89

Gardner, H., 177

General Public License, defined, 169

Google search engine, 6

Graphic artists, 23, 32

Graphics: editing, 46–48; free, 55–56; memory for, 23; PowerPoint animations, 35–37; talking characters, 59–61. *See also* Video clips

Grassi, L. M., 91

Gray, J., 133

H

Half-Baked Software Company, 72

Hancock, S., 72

Harassment, workplace: case study, 151–153; free program on, 183

Hardware: assessment of, 25; required, 5, 23–24

Health care professionals, programs for, 27–29, 186

Help, inexpensive, 129–130, 183–184

Hequet, M., 1

Herrmann, N., 178

Hess, G., 72

Hit counters, 165–166, 175, 183

Hofmann, J., 103

Home pages, student, 106–107

Horton, W., 80

Hosting, 163–164

Hot lists, 66, 67–68

Hot Potatoes software: description of, 72–73; puzzles built with, 94; tracking service, 168

Hot spots: defined, 68; examples of, 69

HTML (HyperText Markup Language) code: defined, 40, 65; in e-mail messages, 52; WYSIWYG tools and, 49, 50–51

HTML editors, 49–50

Hulsmann, T., 127

Hyperlinks, PowerPoint, 34–35

I

Icebreakers, 106–107

Interactive strategies: games, 80–89; puzzles, 94–95; quizzes, 71–80; searches, 89–93; simulations, 96–97; summary on, 97–98

Interactivity tools, free, 58–59

International Society for Performance Improvement, 128

Internet access, 24, 25

Interns, signing on, 130, 183–184

Inventory checklist, 21–23

IRS performance support tool, 122

J

JavaScript code: free, 58; hot spots created with, 68

Jeopardy-type game, 86, 87

Jigsaw puzzles, 94, 95

Job aids: bite-sized, 117; case study, 122–123; defined, 116; EPSS concept, 117; examples of, 120–122; guidelines for choosing, 120; need for, 115–116; summary on, 124; types of, 120; when to use, 118

Just-in-time training, 10, 117

K

Knight, J., 31

Kolb, D., 177

Kruse, K., 137, 143

L

Leadership program: purchased, 183; as typical training event, 115, 116

Learner data, tracking: first considerations in, 164–165; learning management systems for, 169–174; low-cost methods of, 165–167; solutions for, 174–175; summary of, 175–176; test scores, 167–169, 175

Learning, informal, 115, 116

Learning, workflow, 117

Learning Content Management Systems (LCMSs), description of, 174

Learning management systems (LMSs): cost of, 1, 173; free, 4, 169–170; LMS "lite," 170; need for, 169, 175–176; purchasing, 171–174; renting, 170

Learning objects, reusable, 130–133

Learning Site, Macromedia, 52, 169, 175

Learning styles, 177–179

Length of training programs, 13

Licenses: limiting, 153; sharing, 153, 156

Lopuck, L., 32

M

Macintosh users, 4

Macromedia Coursebuilder: description of, 63–64; puzzles built with, 95; as quiz tool, 72

Macromedia Dreamweaver: description of, 50; FTP capability, 164; vendors using, 143

Macromedia Learning Site, 52, 169, 175

Making Sense of Online Learning, 137

Manuals, online, 12

Matching quiz, 73, 78, 79

Mayer, M., 59

McGinnis, M., 172

McKay, J., 117

Media Player, Windows, 25, 62

Metaphors, 65–66

Microphones, 24, 37

Microsoft Agent, 59–61

Microsoft FrontPage, 50–51

Microsoft Notepad, 49–50

Microsoft Office products: Access, 49; Excel, 49, 89; Paint, 46–48; PowerPoint, 32–41, 62, 86–88, 96–97; as required software, 4, 5, 31; support site for, 32; Word, 41–46, 118, 119

Microsoft Producer, 62

Mistakes, costly, 14–15

Moodle learning management system, 170

MovieMaker, Windows, 61–62, 133

Multiple intelligences, theory of, 177–178

Multiple-choice quizzes, 73, 74–76

N

Narration, PowerPoint, 37–39

Needs versus wants, 27–29

NetMeeting software, 103

Networking, 128–129

Notepad, Microsoft, 49–50

O

Off-the-shelf (OTS) products: advantages of, 149–150; buy-versus-build decision, 16–17, 150; criteria for, 150; customizing, 16, 151–153, 180; portal alternative, 156–158; summary on, 158–159; vendors of, 153–156

"101 Tips," game 80–81

Online communities, 52–54, 184, 185

Online training: buy-versus-build decision in, 16–17, 150, 179–182; classroom vs., 10–12; mistakes, 14–15; new thinking for, 12–14

Operating systems, 4, 23, 24–25

Orientation programs: building, 180–182; as typical training events, 115, 116

Outsourced projects: complexity of, 137–138; contracts for, 138, 145–146; cost factors, 139–141; cost-cutting strategies for, 141–142, 144; hidden costs of, 142–143; pricing, 138–139; request for proposal, 143–144; summary on, 147; vendor criteria, 145–146

P

Paint, Microsoft, 46–48

Paper-and-pencil tests, 167, 175

People resources: graphic artists, 23, 32; inventory of, 23; student help, 129–130, 183–184

Performance support tools: bite-sized, 117; case study, 122–123; defined, 116; EPSS concept, 117; examples of, 120–122; need for, 115–116; summary on, 124; types of, 120; when to use, 118

Phone conferencing, 102

Plug-ins, 25, 62

Polls and surveys, 105, 167–168

Portal sites, 156–158

PowerPoint: benefits of, 32; case study, 33; course components, 33; custom-designed Flash vs., 39; games, 86–88; Microsoft Producer and, 62; quizzes, 72; simulations, 96–97; web pages from, 39–41

PowerPoint tools: animations, 35–37; hyperlinks, 34–35; sound effects, 37–39; video clips, 39

Puzzles, 94–95

Q

Quia: class pages, 54; game templates, 83–85; tracking feature, 168

QuickTime player, Apple's, 25, 62

Quiz software: cost of, 80; examples of, 72–73

Quizzes: benefits of, 71; tools for creating, 72–73; types of, 73–79

R

References, vendor, 146

Rehabilitation Act, Section 508 of, 46

Reiser, R., 117

"Relay" game, 81

Repurposing and reusing, 130–133

Request for Proposal (RFP): case study, 144; defined, 143

Resources, leveraging: bartering, 129; networking, 128–129; reusing, 130–133; sharing, 125–128; student help, 129–130, 183–184; summary on, 133

Retirement planning seminars, 115, 116

Richards, G., 132

Rogers, E., 15

Role plays, 111–112, 113

S

Safety training, blended approach to, 182–183

Sales, watching for, 30

Sales training, example of, 184, 186

San Diego State University, 91

Scavenger hunts, 89–90

Scorecard boxes: defined, 5; on e-mail etiquette, 179; on games, 85, 88; on Microsoft Word, 44; on orientation programs, 182; on PowerPoint, 39; on quizzes, 80

SCORM standards, defined, 131

Screen readers, 46

Screen shots, 48

Search activities: treasure hunts, 89–90; web quests, 91–93

Search engines, 6

Search tools, free, 118, 119

Security assessment, 25, 27

Server-side scripting, 166

Seume, D., 126

Sexual harassment training, 183

Shank, P., 137

Shareware, defined, 58

Sharing resources, 125–128

"Shovelware," 143

Simple e-learning programs: building, 31–54; enhancing, 55–69

Simulations, 96–97

Site samplers, 66–67

Site tools, 51–54

Sitze, A., 137

SkillSoft's home page, 157

Slider, Coursebuilder, 63–64

Smith, B., 32

Software: assessment of, 25; Hot Potatoes, 72–73, 94, 168; Macromedia Dreamweaver, 50, 63–64, 72, 143, 164; MS Access, 49; MS Excel, 49, 89; MS FrontPage, 50–51; MS Notepad, 49–50; MS Paint, 46–48; MS PowerPoint, 32–41, 62, 86–88, 96–97; MS Word, 41–46, 118, 119; quiz tools, 72–73, 80; required, 5

Sound effects, PowerPoint, 37–39

Sound Recorder, Windows, 39

Storytelling, 113

Student help, 129–130, 183–184

Student home pages, 106–107

Supervisors, typical training for, 115–116

Survey tools, 105, 167–168, 175

Synchronous collaboration: asynchronous versus, 99–101; defined, 99; tools, 101–103

T

Talking characters, animated, 59–61

Team assignments, 108–110

Technical support, 23, 27

Technology: assessment, 24–27; early adopters of, 15; skills, 4–5, 26

Technology for Trainers, 32

Templates: design, 56–58; game, 82–85

Test scores, 167–169, 175

Themes and metaphors, 65–66

Thiagarajan, S., 80

Thiagi's website, 80

"Tips" e-mail game, 80–81

Toth, T., 32

Tracking learner data: first considerations in, 164–165; learning management systems for, 169–174; low-cost methods of, 165–167; solutions for, 174–175; summary of, 175–176; test scores, 167–169, 175

Training events, typical, 115, 116

Training programs: classroom vs. online, 10–14; just-in-time, 10, 117; learning styles and, 177–179; length of, 13; three examples of, 179–182

Training programs, basic: building, 31–54; enhancing, 55–69

Treasure hunts, 89–90

True-false quizzes, 73, 74

Tutoring, e-, 112–113

U

URLs (Uniform Resource Locators), 54

User considerations, 24–27

V

Vendors: contracts with, 138, 145–146; costs, 138–143, 144; criteria for choosing, 145–146; information for, 140–141; reasons for using, 137–138; request for proposal, 143–144; software used by, 143; summary on, 147

Video clips: case study, 133; cost of, 63; Flash, 62, 133; plug-ins for, 62; PowerPoint, 39; Windows MovieMaker, 61–62

Videoconferencing, 102

Virtual classrooms, 102–103

VoIP (voice over Internet protocol), 102

Volume control, 63

Vox Proxy, 59

Voy Forums, 104

W

Wager, W., 117

Waller, V., 169

Wants versus needs, 27–29

Web conferencing, 102–103

Web design: basic understanding of, 4–5; books on, 32

Web Design for Dummies, 32

Web page templates, free, 56–58

Web Page Wizard, Word's, 41–46

Web quests, 91–93

Webcams, 101

Website, this book's companion, 4, 187

Wikis, defined, 105

Windows 98, 5, 23, 25

Windows environment, 4, 5. *See also* Microsoft Office products

Windows Media Player, 25, 62

Windows MovieMaker, 61–62, 133

Windows XP, 23, 24

Word, Microsoft: accessibility and, 46; Find command, 118, 119; form tools, 44, 45; limitations of, 44; Web Page Wizard Tool, 41–44

Workflow learning, defined, 117

Workplace harassment: case study, 151–153; free program on, 183

WYSIWYG tools: defined, 49; Macromedia Dreamweaver, 50, 143; Microsoft FrontPage, 50–51

X

XML, defined, 65

Y

Yahoo Geocities service, 54

Yahoo Groups, 52, 163, 184

Z

ZEF (Centre for Distance Education), 127

Zoomerang survey tool, 166, 167

About the Author

JANE BOZARTH has been a training practitioner since 1989. A graduate of the University of North Carolina at Chapel Hill, she also has an M.Ed. in training and development/technology in training from North Carolina State University and is pursuing a doctorate in adult education. Her training career began as staff development specialist with the North Carolina Department of Health and Human Services; she then served as training director for the North Carolina Justice Department. Her interest in online learning led to her current position as e-learning coordinator with the North Carolina Office of State Personnel's Human Resources Development Group. Her specialty is finding low-cost ways of creating or purchasing quality e-learning solutions. She is a popular presenter and often appears at national events, such as VNU Learning's Training and Online Learning Conference and Expo and the ASTD International Conference and Expo, as well as many management and professional association gatherings.

In addition to her regular column in *Training Magazine,* Bozarth's work has appeared in trade and academic journals, including the *Creative Training Techniques Newsletter* and the *Journal of Educational Technology and Society.* She can be contacted at jane@bozarthzone.com and at her website, http://www.bozarthzone.com.

Pfeiffer Publications Guide

This guide is designed to familiarize you with the various types of Pfeiffer publications. The formats section describes the various types of products that we publish; the methodologies section describes the many different ways that content might be provided within a product. We also provide a list of the topic areas in which we publish.

FORMATS

In addition to its extensive book-publishing program, Pfeiffer offers content in an array of formats, from fieldbooks for the practitioner to complete, ready-to-use training packages that support group learning.

FIELDBOOK Designed to provide information and guidance to practitioners in the midst of action. Most fieldbooks are companions to another, sometimes earlier, work, from which its ideas are derived; the fieldbook makes practical what was theoretical in the original text. Fieldbooks can certainly be read from cover to cover. More likely, though, you'll find yourself bouncing around following a particular theme, or dipping in as the mood, and the situation, dictate.

HANDBOOK A contributed volume of work on a single topic, comprising an eclectic mix of ideas, case studies, and best practices sourced by practitioners and experts in the field.

An editor or team of editors usually is appointed to seek out contributors and to evaluate content for relevance to the topic. Think of a handbook not as a ready-to-eat meal, but as a cookbook of ingredients that enables you to create the most fitting experience for the occasion.

RESOURCE Materials designed to support group learning. They come in many forms: a complete, ready-to-use exercise (such as a game); a comprehensive resource on one topic (such as conflict management) containing a variety of methods and approaches; or a collection of like-minded activities (such as icebreakers) on multiple subjects and situations.

TRAINING PACKAGE An entire, ready-to-use learning program that focuses on a particular topic or skill. All packages comprise a guide for the facilitator/trainer and a workbook for the participants. Some packages are supported with additional media—such as video—or learning aids, instruments, or other devices to help participants understand concepts or practice and develop skills.

- *Facilitator/trainer's guide* Contains an introduction to the program, advice on how to organize and facilitate the learning event, and step-by-step instructor notes. The guide also contains copies of presentation materials—handouts, presentations, and overhead designs, for example—used in the program.

- *Participant's workbook* Contains exercises and reading materials that support the learning goal and serves as a valuable reference and support guide for participants in the weeks and months that follow the learning event. Typically, each participant will require his or her own workbook.

ELECTRONIC CD-ROMs and Web-based products transform static Pfeiffer content into dynamic, interactive experiences. Designed to take advantage of the searchability, automation, and ease-of-use that technology provides, our e-products bring convenience and immediate accessibility to your workspace.

METHODOLOGIES

CASE STUDY A presentation, in narrative form, of an actual event that has occurred inside an organization. Case studies are not prescriptive, nor are they used to prove a point; they are designed to develop critical analysis and decision-making skills. A case study has a specific time frame, specifies a sequence of events, is narrative in structure, and contains a plot structure—an issue (what should be/have been done?). Use case studies when the goal is to enable participants to apply previously learned theories to the circumstances in the case, decide what is pertinent, identify the real issues, decide what should have been done, and develop a plan of action.

ENERGIZER A short activity that develops readiness for the next session or learning event. Energizers are most commonly used after a break or lunch to stimulate or refocus the group. Many involve some form of physical activity, so they are a useful way to counter post-lunch lethargy. Other uses include transitioning from one topic to another, where "mental" distancing is important.

EXPERIENTIAL LEARNING ACTIVITY (ELA) A facilitator-led intervention that moves participants through the learning cycle from experience to application (also known as a Structured Experience). ELAs are carefully thought-out designs in which there is a definite learning purpose and intended outcome. Each step—everything that participants do during the activity—facilitates the accomplishment of the stated goal. Each ELA includes complete instructions for facilitating the intervention and a clear statement of goals, suggested group size and timing, materials required, an explanation of the process, and, where appropriate, possible variations to the activity. (For more detail on Experiential Learning Activities, see the Introduction to the *Reference Guide to Handbooks and Annuals*, 1999 edition, Pfeiffer, San Francisco.)

GAME A group activity that has the purpose of fostering team spirit and togetherness in addition to the achievement of a pre-stated goal. Usually contrived—undertaking a desert expedition, for example—this type of learning method offers an engaging means for participants to demonstrate and practice business and interpersonal skills. Games are effective for team building and personal development mainly because the goal is subordinate to the process—the means through which participants reach decisions, collaborate, communicate, and generate trust and understanding. Games often engage teams in "friendly" competition.

ICEBREAKER A (usually) short activity designed to help participants overcome initial anxiety in a training session and/or to acquaint the participants with one another. An icebreaker can be a fun activity or can be tied to specific topics or training goals. While a useful tool in itself, the icebreaker comes into its own in situations where tension or resistance exists within a group.

INSTRUMENT A device used to assess, appraise, evaluate, describe, classify, and summarize various aspects of human behavior. The term used to describe an instrument depends primarily on its format and purpose. These terms include survey, questionnaire, inventory, diagnostic, survey, and poll. Some uses of instruments include providing instrumental feedback to group members, studying here-and-now processes or functioning within a group, manipulating group composition, and evaluating outcomes of training and other interventions.

Instruments are popular in the training and HR field because, in general, more growth can occur if an individual is provided with a method for focusing specifically on his or her own behavior. Instruments also are used to obtain information that will serve as a basis for change and to assist in workforce planning efforts.

Paper-and-pencil tests still dominate the instrument landscape with a typical package comprising a facilitator's guide, which offers advice on administering the instrument and interpreting the collected data, and an initial set of instruments. Additional instruments are available separately. Pfeiffer, though, is investing heavily in e-instruments. Electronic instrumentation provides effortless distribution and, for larger groups particularly, offers advantages over paper-and-pencil tests in the time it takes to analyze data and provide feedback.

LECTURETTE A short talk that provides an explanation of a principle, model, or process that is pertinent to the participants' current learning needs. A lecturette is intended to establish a common language bond between the trainer and the participants by providing a mutual frame of reference. Use a lecturette as an introduction to a group activity or event, as an interjection during an event, or as a handout.

MODEL A graphic depiction of a system or process and the relationship among its elements. Models provide a frame of reference and something more tangible, and more easily remembered, than a verbal explanation. They also give participants something to "go on," enabling them to track their own progress as they experience the dynamics, processes, and relationships being depicted in the model.

ROLE PLAY A technique in which people assume a role in a situation/scenario: a customer service rep in an angry-customer exchange, for example. The way in which the role is approached is then discussed and feedback is offered. The role play is often repeated using a different approach and/or incorporating changes made based on feedback received. In other words, role playing is a spontaneous interaction involving realistic behavior under artificial (and safe) conditions.

SIMULATION A methodology for understanding the interrelationships among components of a system or process. Simulations differ from games in that they test or use a model that depicts or mirrors some aspect of reality in form, if not necessarily in content. Learning occurs by studying the effects of change on one or more factors of the model. Simulations are commonly used to test hypotheses about what happens in a system—often referred to as "what if?" analysis—or to examine best-case/worst-case scenarios.

THEORY A presentation of an idea from a conjectural perspective. Theories are useful because they encourage us to examine behavior and phenomena through a different lens.

TOPICS

The twin goals of providing effective and practical solutions for workforce training and organization development and meeting the educational needs of training and human resource professionals shape Pfeiffer's publishing program. Core topics include the following:

Leadership & Management

Communication & Presentation

Coaching & Mentoring

Training & Development

e-Learning

Teams & Collaboration

OD & Strategic Planning

Human Resources

Consulting

What will you find on pfeiffer.com?

- The best in workplace performance solutions for training and HR professionals

- Downloadable training tools, exercises, and content

- Web-exclusive offers

- Training tips, articles, and news

- Seamless online ordering

- Author guidelines, information on becoming a Pfeiffer Affiliate, and much more

Discover more at www.pfeiffer.com

Customer Care

Have a question, comment, or suggestion? Contact us! We value your feedback and we want to hear from you.

For questions about this or other Pfeiffer products, you may contact us by:

E-mail: **customer@wiley.com**

Mail: **Customer Care Wiley/Pfeiffer**
         10475 Crosspoint Blvd.
         Indianapolis, IN 46256

Phone: **(US) 800-274-4434** (Outside the US: 317-572-3985)

Fax: **(US) 800-569-0443** (Outside the US: 317-572-4002)

To order additional copies of this title or to browse other Pfeiffer products, visit us online at **www.pfeiffer.com**.

For **Technical Support** questions, call **800-274-4434.**

For authors guidelines, log on to www.pfeiffer.com and click on "Resources for Authors."

If you are . . .

A **college bookstore, a professor, an instructor, or work in higher education** and you'd like to place an order or request an exam copy, please contact jbreview@wiley.com.

A **general retail bookseller** and you'd like to establish an account or speak to a local sales representative, contact Melissa Grecco at 201-748-6267 or mgrecco@wiley.com.

An **exclusively online bookseller**, contact Amy Blanchard at 530-756-9456 or ablanchard @wiley.com or Jennifer Johnson at 206-568-3883 or jjohnson@wiley.com, both of our Online Sales department.

A **librarian or library representative**, contact John Chambers in our Library Sales department at 201-748-6291 or jchamber@wiley.com.

A **reseller, training company/consultant, or corporate trainer**, contact Charles Regan in our Special Sales department at 201-748-6553 or cregan@wiley.com.

A **specialty retail distributor** (includes specialty gift stores, museum shops, and corporate bulk sales), contact Kim Hendrickson in our Special Sales department at 201-748-6037 or khendric@wiley.com.

Purchasing for the **Federal government**, contact Ron Cunningham in our Special Sales department at 317-572-3053 or rcunning@wiley.com.

Purchasing for a **State or Local government**, contact Charles Regan in our Special Sales department at 201-748-6553 or cregan@wiley.com.